"THE" DIET FOR YOUR MIND
TO HELP YOU FIND
THE TRUTH
THAT WILL SET YOU FREE

"THE" SPIRITUAL, "THE" MIND, DIET

By

MINISTER OSCAR G. SETTLE

© 2010 by MINISTER OSCAR G. SETTLE. All rights reserved.

No part of this book may be reproduced, stored in a retrieval system, or transmitted by any means, electronic, mechanical, photocopying, recording, or otherwise, without written permission from the author.

First published by AuthorHouse 09/30/10

ISBN: 978-1-4184-6061-7 (e)
ISBN: 978-1-4184-1681-2 (sc)
ISBN: 978-1-4184-1682-9 (hc)

Library of Congress Control Number: 2004090610

This book is printed on acid-free paper.

Printed in the United States of America
Bloomington, IN

CONTENTS

FORWARD vii

INTRODUCTION ix

THE DIET 1

THE MIND 4

THE MIND AND DIET 7

THE HOLY BIBLE (THE MANUAL) 8

MY, YOUR, HIS, HERS OR ITS STUFF (SMORGASBORD) 10

THE TRUTH: (WHAT IS TRUTH? AND WHERE DO I FIND TRUTH? THE TRUTH THAT WILL MAKE ME FREE) 13

THE BATTLE BETWEEN LIES AND THE TRUTH 18

WISDOM KNOWLEDGE AND "HOLY" UNDERSTANDING.... 21

IN THE IMAGE AND LIKENESS OF GOD 28

THE TRINITY OF GOD: 31

    FIRST PERSON (GOD THE FATHER) *31*

    SECOND PERSON (GOD THE SON, JESUS) *32*

    THIRD PERSON (GOD THE HOLY SPIRIT) *33*

TWO DISPENSATIONS (INNOCENCE AND CONSCIENCE).... 36

THE TRINITY OF HUMANITY 38

    1. MAN AS A SPIRIT 38

    2. MAN AS THE BODY 38

    3. MAN AS THE SOUL 39

A SOUL TO BE SAVED 42

SIN AND SINS 45

WHO IS SATAN? 48

THE TRINITY OF EVIL: 49

    FIRST PERSON (LUCIFER) 49

    SECOND PERSON (SATAN) 50

    THIRD PERSON (THE DEVIL) 52

SUMMARY OF THE TRINITY OF EVIL 56

THE TRINITY OF CONSCIOUSNESSES 58

    1. GOD-CONSCIOUSNESS (SPIRIT AND MIND) 60

    2. WORLD-CONSCIOUSNESS (BODY AND FIVE SENSES) 61

    THE SIXTH SENSE (THE HOLY SPIRIT) 62

    3. SELF-CONSCIOUSNESS (HEART: AFFECTIONS) 62

THE INTERACTION OF THE TRI-UNITY OF CONSCIOUSNESS 64

YOUR PERSONAL COMPUTER OF MAN (P.C.M.) AND YOUR PERSONAL COMPUTER OF GOD (P.C.S.) 67

THE MIND AND THE COMPUTER 70

THE SECOND BIRTH (BORN-AGAIN) 72

HOW TO BE BORN A SECOND TIME (BORN-AGAIN) 80

THE NEW COVENANT 85

THE CHRISTIAN TRINITY: (THE FRUIT OF THE SPIRIT) 92

    1. FAITH *92*

    2. HOPE *94*

    RELATIONSHIPS: (THE FAMILY, THE CHURCH) *97*

    3. LOVE (DESSERT) *101*

LOVE AND RELATIONSHIPS 103

INTRODUCTION TO THE DESSERT 105

WHAT IS LOVE? 110

THE DEFINING ELEMENTS OF LOVE 115

    1. GIVING *115*

    2. FORGIVING *119*

    FORGIVING GOD *120*

    3. UNDERSTANDING *124*

THE ESSENCE OF LOVE 128

LOVE AND LIKE 132

FIRST CORINTHIANS THIRTEEN 141

WHAT'S LOVE GOT TO DO WITH IT? 150

BROTHERLY AND DIVINE LOVE 160

    A. BROTHERLY LOVE 163

    B. DIVINE LOVE (LOVING GOD) 166

MALE-FEMALE! HUSBAND-WIFE! AND LOVE 170

    1-FRIENDSHIP 170

    2-FRANKNESS 174

    3-FIDELITY 179

    4-FORGIVENESS 183

    5-FAITH 190

PARENT-CHILD LOVE 195

IS LOVE A STRENGTH OR WEAKNESS? 202

CONCLUSION 207

FOOTNOTES AND SOURCES 212

FORWARD

I will take this opportunity to thank all of those who have assisted with this writing. Those who have edited, typed, prayed, or contributed in any way to the completion of this writing, I thank you and employ God's blessings on you.

Finally, to those of you who have purchased and propose to read the following words, I pray for God's blessing of wisdom and knowledge upon you. Furthermore, I pray that you enjoy reading these words as much as you would enjoy eating a gourmet meal. Thus, if you arrive at a chapter or section and you cannot mentally accept or digest what is presented, your mind diet is not ready; please don't suffer indigestion. Rather, place the chapter or section in the "frig" (keep it, don't throw it away) because tomorrow, or tomorrow's tomorrow, it probably will be just what you need to place your mind on a diet to find the truth that will set you free.

INTRODUCTION
(SOUP DU JOUR)

There must be a coming together of thoughts and a mutual understanding if we are to travel through the following pages together and on one accord.

Therefore, I will introduce myself as an ordained minister; licensed to preach the Gospel of Jesus Christ.

If you are a Christian, then I greet you, my brother or sister, in the name of our Lord and Savior Jesus Christ.

If you have not been born-again, I greet you as a future brother or sister, in the name of our Lord and Savior Jesus Christ.

I believe that men under the guidance of the Holy Spirit wrote the Holy Bible. What? If we believe that the spirit of the prince of the air can cause a man, or woman, to perform an act – "The devil made me do it" – then why do we not believe that the Spirit of the breath of life can "Make me, him, her or it, do it"?

In the Holy Bible,[1] in the first chapter of the first book, this Holy Writ declares that God created the heaven and the earth. The Word goes on to say that on the sixth day, He created man.

In the second chapter the creative act is explained in further detail. The Holy Writ says man was created from the dust of the ground, and after the breath of life was breathed into his nostrils, man became a living soul.

The first man, or living soul, was called Adam. God, finding it wasn't good for man to be alone, created a companion for Adam. God took a rib from Adam's body and created a wife for Adam, and she was called Eve.

God, being a good father, gave the newlyweds property and wealth as a wedding gift. They were given an entire estate called "The Garden of Eden." The Lord God planted all sorts of beautiful trees in the garden, trees producing the choicest of fruit for food. God gave them a diet to follow. The diet consisted of the fruit of every tree in the garden with one exception. In the middle of the garden were the Tree of Life, and the Tree of Conscience, giving knowledge of good and evil (bad). The Tree of Conscience was the tree God told them not to eat of, which was planted in the middle of the garden. Adam was informed that if he ate of the fruit of the Tree of Conscience, in other words if he included this tree in his diet; he would die. Later we will see that the death that would result from the fruit of the tree would be physical and spiritual.

Yes, you are right. Adam and Eve ate of the Tree of Conscience. Thus, they left their diet as was planned for them. Therefore, since the first man ate of the forbidden fruit, or received a conscience of good and evil (bad), then the seed of humanity became infected, contaminated. So, to rid humanity of the conscience of evil, there had to be an antidote, to enter the blood of man to free man from the contamination. So, this transfusion calls for the blood of Jesus to be transferred to a person, to set him or her free from evil. The transfusion does not physically enter the physical body of a person; rather through the spirit it wipes away the contamination, thereby allowing the person an avenue to become free from sin.

> So Jesus said it again, "With all the earnestness I posses I tell you this: unless you eat the flesh of the Messiah and drink his blood, you cannot have eternal life within you. But anyone who does eat my flesh and drink my blood has eternal life, and I will raise him at the Last Day. For my flesh is the true food, and my blood is the true drink. Everyone who eats my flesh and drinks my blood is in me, and I in him. I live by the power of the living Father who sent me, and in the same way those who partake of me shall live because of me. I am the true Bread from heaven; and anyone who eats this Bread shall live forever, and not die as your fathers did though they ate bread from heaven."
> (St John 6:53-58 TLB)[2]

Then after the transfusion, there has to be a change from within. The change is needed because the antidote will only work by faith in the antidote. The faith comes by hearing what the antidote says. Since, the contaminated seed of a person is still within, a battle is started. The battle takes place in the mind. The mind will respond in a way that is good or evil according to the programming of the mind. Programming by the good is possible because God made the mind.

The mind is also capable of evil because of contamination. So, to make the mind good, there must be a diet, a diet for the mind.

> It seems to be a fact of life that when I want to do what is right, I inevitably do what is wrong. I love to do God's will so far as my new nature is concerned; but there is something else deep within me, in my lower nature, that is at war with my mind and wins the fight and makes me a slave to the sin that is still within me. In my mind I want to be God's willing servant but instead I find myself still enslaved to sin.
>
> So you see how it is: my new life tells me to do right, but the old nature that is still inside me loves to sin. Oh, what a terrible predicament I'm in! Who will free me from my slavery to this lower nature? Thank God! It has been done by Jesus Christ our Lord. He has set me free. (Romans 7:21-25 TLB)

One observation I have made is that once you have begun to understand the spiritual side of existence, you will notice that there is always something in the physical that will help you understand the spiritual. When Jesus would seek to enlighten his disciples or a crowd, He would use a physical illustration to communicate a spiritual principle. Furthermore, if he were speaking to farmers, His physical illustration would be about the physical seed. So He would teach about the spiritual harvest and the Kingdom of God. If fishermen were in His midst, then He would speak of physical fishing, to teach the same lesson about the Kingdom of God.

I believe that our Lord and Savior used this method in the effort to take a known (knowledge of the physical) to teach an unknown (knowledge of the spiritual). Thus, many of his teachings were through what are called parables.

> Again, the kingdom of heaven is like unto treasure hid in a field; the which when a man hath found, he hideth, and for joy thereof goeth and selleth all that he hath, and buyeth that field. (St. Matthew 13:44)
>
> All things are lawful for me, but all things are not expedient: all things are lawful for me, but all things edify not. (I Corinthians 10:23)

In recognition of the Lord's method, the Holy Spirit has taught me to look at the physical to find and understand the spiritual. Thus, as the physical presents many foods which are edible, I have learned that if I am to avoid damage to the physical body, I have to watch what I eat as well as how much I eat; I need a diet. So, if the eating of the physical forbidden fruit resulted in my having to place my physical body on a diet, then I must also place my spiritual life, mind, on a diet. Remember, the original diet didn't cause physical or spiritual problems. It was the inclusion of the forbidden fruit that caused the need for a physical and spiritual diet. Furthermore, whether we speak of a physical or spiritual diet, the beginning has to be with the mind. So, if I want to follow a physical diet or a spiritual diet, I'll begin with an intangible, a spiritual thing – the mind. The mind is programmed to know that there are all kinds of food out there for the physical body and spiritual mind. However, with a good diet, I'll know the truth that will place my freedom of consumption on the diet to help me find the truth that makes me free.

THE DIET

Recently I found that I was not pleased with my physical appearance. I had gained weight and my clothes were not fitting my body as I desired. My stomach had begun to hang over the waist of my pants, my pants were wearing out between the legs because my thighs had gotten too large. The bottoms of my tapered fitting shirts would pop off while I was wearing them. So, I went on a physical diet to reduce my physical weight and save money on repairs to the seat of my pants and also to avoid having to purchase larger clothes.

I noticed one of my co-workers had reduced her weight. One day I asked her how she had accomplished her weight reduction. She gave me a book that she had been using for dieting for the physical body. I was amazed that the author emphasized so much that to change the body, one had to change the mind. The thought life (the mind), along with a thought life that considered consumption of food, was the key to her diet.

The author stated that if one was to change one's physical appearance, one had to change one's thoughts toward food. The type and amount of food consumed had to be considered. In other words, if one wanted to lose physical pounds or inches, one had to change the mind to consume less food. The type of food and how and when it was consumed, had to be thought about and changed.

I made one further observation about her approach. This was not a quick-fix diet. The change in the mind would be the key to the loss of weight. Thus, since a change in the mind was needed to be successful, the results would prevent the common fault of a quick-fix diet – the return of the weight.

Since successfully losing the pounds and inches, I have noticed a part of my natural thought (mind) process is concern with what physical food I consumed and how much and when. The process has developed because I have placed my mind, along with my physical body, on the diet. Therefore, I have come to realize that if one is to have a well-adjusted physical body, one must diet (be observant of what and how much is consumed). Hence, to have a well-adjusted mind, there must be observance of what and how much is consumed mentally. In other words, there is a need for a diet for the mind.

The problem that immediately surfaces is how to put the mind on a diet. Where do I get the food for the mind? What is good for the mind? How can I tell if I need a diet for my mind? After all, especially here in America, where freedom of thought and expression are of paramount importance, why even consider a limitation on my thought life?

With the physical body, I can turn to medical science to determine if a physical diet is needed. There is a medical chart that shows if I am a certain height and have a certain build (frame) what my physical weight should be. Mirrors, friends, and a change in clothes size can indicate that I need to go on a physical diet. But, what indicators or signs am I to observe in order to know when a mind diet is needed?

Furthermore, to accomplish a physical diet, I can do sit-ups. I can jog and do other physicals exercises to meet my goal. I can count calories, eat less fat, and sodium to aid my quest for physical weight reduction. But, how is the mental diet accomplished? Also, who says, or has the right to say, when my mind needs to be placed on a diet?

When I began to consider my physical diet, I searched for a diet that would include a mental as well as a physical change. I considered finding a diet that the author had developed for himself or herself, not a diet that was based on the author's vicarious experiences. Rather, I sought a diet that was created by the author from the author's personal experience. The idea was that if he or she had created the diet from personal experiences, then he or she would know from experience what the diet would do and what it would not do. It would be a diet from someone who had been there, done that.

This approach was founded upon the theory, belief, that he or she who made it knows what's best for it. When my Buick car needs repairing, I carry the car to the Buick dealer. When my Whirlpool dishwasher is broken, Whirlpool is called to do the repairs. When my stereo entertainment component, made by Zenith, went mono, I went to R.C.A., who directed me to Zenith. I went to Sears, some years ago, to have my stove repaired, only to be informed that Sears only services what it sells or what it makes. Thus, there seems to be a rule

THE DIET

of life, which is consistent with each of the examples above. That rule is that he or she who made it knows best how to fix it.

When approaching a diet for the mind, we first have to recognize that the mind is intangible and has a spiritual existence. Next, there must be a decision on who made the mind.

I believe that God made the person and the mind. This is said in the Holy Bible, which was written by physical men who were under the spiritual guidance of the Holy Spirit.

> And God said, Let us make man in our image, after our likeness:.....
>
> ...So God created man in his own image, in the image of God created he him; male and female created he them. (Genesis 1:26,27)

"THE" DIET FOR YOUR MIND TO HELP YOU FIND THE TRUTH THAT WILL SET YOU FREE

THE MIND

I must admit that I had a slight problem with understanding the brain and mind concept. As many students of the Holy Bible once believed that the soul and spirit were one, the same conclusion about the brain and mind has some confused. All right, I was one of these students. I observe that when one refers to the brain one is usually talking about the mind, and thereby using the two synonymously. After all isn't it the mind we often refer to in speaking of the brain? Someone would say that another had a bad mind and immediately the conclusion would be drawn that there was a problem with the brain. So, when I was a child, I thought as a child. However, thanks to the Holy Spirit I have knowledge of the Holy. Thus, I have learned a truth that has made me free. Free from what, you may ask? My reply is free from spiritual ignorance.

In the Webster's Dictionary[1] the brain is defined as:

> The portion of the vertebrate central nervous system that constitutes the organ of thought and neural coordination, includes all the higher nervous centers receiving stimuli from the sense organs and interpreting and correlating them to formulate the motor impulses, is made up of neurons and supporting and nutritive structures, is enclosed within the skull, and is continuous with the spinal cord through the foramen magnum. (1): intellect, mind,

Webster says the mind is:

> The element or complex of elements in an individual that feels, perceives, thinks, wills, and especially reasons: the conscious mental events and capabilities in an organism: the organized conscious and unconscious adaptive mental activity of an organism.

Again, we can conclude that the brain is the mainframe, where all the thought process goes on. Whereas, the mind is the results of the brain – the five senses, the emotions and responses. So, even though it is the brain that receives all data, stores all data, and releases all data, through its programmers, the five senses, it is the mind that will determine the emotions and responses to the data. Thus, again, it's the totality of the person that is arrived at through the brain that makes the mind.

Will we not say later that the "SOUL" is the totality of a person? Now we are saying that the "MIND" is the totality of the person. It appears that we are in a similar conclusion as we were with the brain and the mind or, as we will see later, the spirit and the soul.

When we compare the definitions given for the soul and mind, there is an appearance of the two being synonymous. However, a closer evaluation of the soul and the mind will reveal the difference between them.

Let us do a quick review of our conclusions. First, the mind is aligned with the spirit of the person. The heart is aligned with the soul of the person. The mind and heart are intangibles. The mind and soul only have knowledge of the world by way of the physical body. The physical body is where God-consciousness and self-consciousness have knowledge of the physical, world-consciousness. Thus, the receipt of what is happening in the world that will be passed to the spirit, or intangibles, will determine the response of the heart. The response of the heart, emotions, affections and so on, will depend on the brain. A brain which is programmed (set) to the world will lead to a mind programmed by and for the world. A world-programmed brain will feed the mind on the world and self, leaving the God program out. The brain's conclusion will be the programming of the mind. What is done with information received will be the thought life of the person. This thought life is called the mind. The heart, which is made up of emotions and responses from the mind, gives evidence of the mind and the direction of the soul.

The soul does consist of affection, emotions, desires and so on. However, it is the mind that feeds the soul. The mind will determine the emotions, desires, feelings and affections. So, in the mind of a person can be found the data that will determine the emotions, affections and so on, but the mind in receipt of data from the brain will determine what conscious decision will be made. Thus, the

"THE" DIET FOR YOUR MIND TO HELP YOU FIND THE TRUTH THAT WILL SET YOU FREE

response to what is seen, heard, and spoken will determine the essence, mind, or soul of a person.

Maybe a simple illustration could be used to better understand the soul and mind. A very angry Sam hit Bob because he and Bob had a disagreement. The five senses responded. There was a sense of seeing Sam hit him and a sense of Sam's loud cologne. Then the sense of taste was present because of the blood in Bob's mouth. With his sense of hearing, Bob heard the foul words spoken by Sam. Finally, there was the sense of feeling because pain registered in the area where Sam hit him.

The brain received the messages from the five senses. Then Bob's brain thought what to do. His brain, in its effort to decide the response to Sam's aggressiveness, sent the information to the programmer, the mind. The mind, programmed to fight, went into self-consciousness. In Bob's emotions, desires, and self-will – his soul – he made the decision to do unto Sam as Sam had done unto him.

Now let us take the same scenario with Sam and Bob, but on this occasion Bob had his mind on a diet. All of Bob's senses give the same information to the brain. The brain releases the information to the mind. The mind, receiving the information from the five senses (world-consciousness) decides to ask, "What would Jesus do?"

Pray for the happiness of those who curse you,
implore God's blessings on those who hurt you.
If someone slaps you on one cheek, let him slap the
other too! ....(St. Luke 6:28-29 TLB)

Thus, Bob's mind was trained in, and focused upon, God-consciousness. Being trained in God-consciousness, Bob's mind turned the other cheek. Thus, it is not the heart that needs to be placed on a diet, even though it will be the heart that benefits from the diet. Rather it is the mind that feeds the heart which needs the diet.

.......FOR AS HE THINKETH IN HIS HEART, SO IS HE:....... (PROVERBS 23:7)

THE MIND AND DIET

As I stated before, I desired a change in my physical appearance. I recognized a co-worker who had accomplished the weight loss she desired. Next, I approached the co-worker to ask her how she reached her desire. She referred me to a book, which she has consulted to guide her in accomplishing the results that I could see. This book was her manual, and later came to be my manual, to tell her and me what, how and when to perform certain tasks that would eventually bring about the desired results.

Man, in performing in the image of God, in creating, will develop a manual to be consulted, used, in man's effort to understand the creation of man. If a person buys a VCR, it will come with different types of instructions. There will be instructions on connecting the VCR to the television. Inasmuch as most homes have cable service, the written instructions will give instructions on VCR and cable connection with the television. There will be written instructions to aid the best existence of the creation that the creator knows. In the case of dieting, there will be instructions on how to reach the goal of losing weight.

Surely, if the creation of God, man, knows how to instruct his (man's) creation, would not the creator of man give man instructions on life, since God created man's life? The answer, even without going into deductive reasoning, has to be yes. As the book received from my co-worker was used as my manual to diet and lose weight, I have located a manual from God to put my mind on a diet.

"THE" DIET FOR YOUR MIND TO HELP YOU FIND THE TRUTH THAT WILL SET YOU FREE

THE HOLY BIBLE
(THE MANUAL)

Before I go any further, I believe that it is necessary to address something here: in an attempt to find a diet for the body – the physical – one can find several manuals prepared for weight loss. Furthermore, the same is true with the mind's (spiritual) diet. There is the Koran that is used by one group, the Torah that is used by another group, and the Holy Bible, which is consulted by this writer and many others.

The three largest religious groups of people use these three manuals. Furthermore, each manual has a spiritual diet. Some instructions are the same but there are more instructions that are different. The purpose of this writing is not to say which is right or which is wrong. However, I will share why the Holy Bible was chosen to be my manual, instead of the Koran or the Torah.

The Koran did not become this writer's manual because it is based upon the teaching of a man, whose knowledge was received from God, whereas, the Holy Bible's teachings are based upon God, who took the form of a physical man.

The Torah would be all right if I was seeking only to know a part of a mental diet. An analogy would be a search for knowledge on how to lose weight in the abdominal area. It would be all right if I only wanted to know what's in the old will. Now, the Holy Bible contains an Old Testament and a New Testament; an additional amount of information, the up-to-date information and a complete manual.

So, since I was trying to accomplish a total diet, I went to the manual that was prepared for the same. One more word here in reference to a diet: the Holy Bible used by Christians prescribes a way of life, not just a religion. The Christians do recognize Jehovah God as a deity. However, they go beyond a mere worshiping of a deity and seek understanding of the Creator's manual so that they can have and live life according to the manual. Remember, as I said before, the physical diet I chose also required a mental change, which would allow not only for losing weight, but also for keeping the weight off. So, to have a successful physical change, there is a need for a mental change, a change in one's way of life. Then, how much more is there

THE HOLY BIBLE (THE MANUAL)

a need to change the mind? This is one more reason for my manual being the Holy Bible.

With the mentioning of religion, I believe I must address something before going any further. There is a thought out there, in cyber space, that all religion is a falsehood. Thus, even when the Holy Bible is presented as "The" Manual, there is a response that it was written by man. In anticipation that some would believe this, and since there will always be the skeptics, I can only share with you what The Manual itself says.

The Holy Bible (the Manual) states that man wrote the words of the Holy Bible, but the writing was under the inspiration and guidance of God.

>All scripture is given by inspiration of God, and is profitable for doctrine, for reproof, for correction, for instruction in righteousness: (2 Timothy 3:16)

"THE" DIET FOR YOUR MIND TO HELP YOU FIND THE TRUTH THAT WILL SET YOU FREE

MY, YOUR, HIS, HERS OR ITS STUFF (SMORGASBORD)

Then there are some who will disregard all manuals, with the attitude that you should not believe in that stuff. Well, believe it or not, every living human being believes in some stuff. In life there is a smorgasbord of stuff, whether its God's or just the regular old human (physical) stuff. After all, that's how we exist: on stuff. The physical body needs foodstuff. The spiritual needs spiritual stuff. So, whether a person believes in my stuff, your stuff, his, hers, or its stuff, it's impossible to exist without believing in something or somebody's stuff.

Thus, the question is not whether one believes in stuff, but rather which stuff or whose stuff. As one begins to consider a diet for the mind "stuff," one should study different stuff. Yes, I am encouraging you to learn about as much stuff as possible. After all, this is how I arrived at, and accepted, Jesus' "stuff." I studied Islam, the Koran, Judaism, the Torah, and some of the leading scholars and thinkers' stuff, and I learned something from all of them.

From my studies of Islam and other eastern stuff, I learned how to meditate, relax and get to know the true me.

Through my exploration of Judaism, I learned who made the thing inside me that would receive stuff. I learned that because of my earthly parents (Adam and Eve), bad stuff was out there which could damage or contaminate my mind.

Then I was led to and studied the Christian "stuff." The Christian stuff informed me that He who had made my mind had recognized that a contamination, a virus, had entered the mind. Then he sent workers to fix the damage caused by the contamination. The creator of the contamination had many allies, allies who were constantly releasing the viruses or contamination to cause continuous damage and to create within the mind the belief that there was no hope of recovery.

As I continued to study the Christian stuff, I learned that the creator of me had decided that if you want something done right, you must do it yourself. So, this C.E.O. packed his bags and left his palace

MY, YOUR, HIS, HERS OR ITS STUFF (SMORGASBORD)

and took on the clothing of flesh, the same as those He was going to help, and arrived on earth to repair the mind. However, when He arrived He didn't receive the best palace. He wasn't accommodated at the greatest palace on earth, but the opposite.

You see, when it was time to appear on earth, He who had made the earth, and all of its inhabitants, was told that there was no room at any palace or inn. Well, I gather that your mind can explore the idea of creating a place, and all that dwells therein, and arriving for a visit and being turned away by the best palace as well as the worst inn. And you can explore how you would feel if you had to be born in a stable with straw as your mattress and animals as your housemates.

Then, to add insult to injury, so to speak, to His visit to earth, the race in which you claim your heritage turns against you. You brought to your race grace, but they desired to continue under the law. You know the way to life, but many including your own race, will not follow you. You, being the truth, but they will not listen to the truth. You made life, and had come to give life more abundantly, but most chose death and eventually did take your life.

I said to myself, "Now this is good stuff!" I will seek to learn more about this Christian stuff. Learning about the Christian stuff, not just because of the claim that He made me, but so that I could learn about my physical and spiritual existence, I would study His life, His way, and His truth. Why? you may ask. This Jesus had taught me more in just reading about His pre-birth and birth than any other character I had studied. Furthermore, I studied President George Washington's life to understand American History, so why not study the one who made all history.

From His birth, He had shown me that life wouldn't be easy. Yet, He didn't give up, or use the power of the physical sword to accomplish his objective. Even though he made the earth, making him a king of the earthly kingdom, He accepted his place of birth and lived a life of an ordinary man. Every contamination used by His enemies could have been conceived as sour grapes. However, each time He took the sour grapes and made wine. After making the wine, he invited all to come to the feast and enter His kingdom, especially his kinsmen.

"THE" DIET FOR YOUR MIND TO HELP YOU FIND THE TRUTH THAT WILL SET YOU FREE

The invitation went out to the world, to whosoever would, to come and drink and eat of his feast. The feast activities would feed not only the body, but also the soul. Then once you ate at the feast, you would become a new person. The old things would pass away and a new you would become alive. The old me, with contaminations, would not be renewed. Rather, as a feast participant, I would become a new person. The five senses would be renewed. I would see with new eyes, hear with new ears and so on. I would be washed and made clean. Then I would be introduced to His father.

The more I read The Manual, the more I began to realize that this was not only good stuff but also the right stuff, the best stuff. It was the stuff to remove the virus from my mind and create within me a clean heart and a saved soul.

This stuff, this Jesus Stuff, allows my fellow person and me to treat each other as equals. The stuff says to not only love my friends, but love my enemy. The stuff says if I have eyes trained in this stuff, I won't see male or female, Jew or Gentile, race, creed or color, rich or poor, only fellow persons. Then when I see fellow-persons, I see persons who are like me, born-again, and children of God, and those who differ only in having one birth, God's children.

Now, this is out of this world stuff. This stuff had shown me the way to the truth and the life. The Christian stuff had identified who made heaven, earth and me. At last I could understand why I had ups and downs. I could understand why I sought to destroy and not build. Also I could understand why I wanted to do right, but ended up doing wrong. The mind wanted to do right, but something would cause me to do wrong. The Christian stuff had shown me the curse. However, there was still some doubt whether the Christian stuff was not just good stuff but the true stuff.

THE TRUTH:
(WHAT IS TRUTH? AND WHERE DO I FIND TRUTH?
THE TRUTH THAT WILL MAKE ME FREE)

> Pilate therefore said unto him, Art thou a king then? Jesus answered, Thou sayest that I am a king. To this end was I born, and for this cause came I into the world, that I should bear witness unto the truth. Everyone that is of the truth heareth my voice. Pilate saith unto him, What is truth? . . . . .(St. John 18:37-38)
>
> Then said Jesus to those Jews which believed on him, If ye continue in my word, then are ye my disciples indeed; And ye shall know the truth, and the truth shall make you free. (St. John 8:31-32)

When I entered the ministry, I would often encourage others to read the Holy Bible, The Manual, to find the truth. Often I was confronted with the question, what is truth? Furthermore, why is what's in the Bible considered truth. They would continue with the statement that men wrote the Bible. Who is to say that the Bible contains the truth? Who can say that one man's word should be believed as the truth over another man's word?

Then there were the females who would say that the Bible always speaks of the male gender being the head of the house, the family, and even the church. Their conclusion was that the Bible written by man was only for man. Next they would say the females in the Bible, starting with Eve, were often used to portray the negative. So, why should a book written and produced by males and staring males even be considered by females as the truth.

I would try to respond to these responses with words from the Holy Bible. Then I remembered what my fifth grade teacher taught me. That is, you cannot define a word with the word. Thus, as I attempted to give a scripture response, I found myself in the fifth grade again.

I pondered these thoughts of others, accepting the point that the Bible was written by men. It did contain negative things about women

"THE" DIET FOR YOUR MIND TO HELP YOU FIND THE TRUTH THAT WILL SET YOU FREE

and this did pose the question why the Holy Bible should be the truth. Yes, I read the above scripture that said men, under the inspiration of the Holy Spirit, wrote all scripture. However, again I was in essence using the word of God to say the word is truth.

I became more concerned now. Not only could I not give an adequate answer to the truth issue; a statement made to me came to mind. "Truth is like beauty, it's in the eye of the beholder. There is not one truth, but many truths." The statement that there are many truths about many things I could accept, but I couldn't accept that there couldn't be a truth about one thing. There were truths about single things, such as the truth that a normal hand has five extensions. Whether you say you have four fingers and one thumb, or lump them together and say you have five fingers, there would be on a normal hand five extensions.

Well, needless to say, I found myself accepting these responses as the truth. In other words in my effort to communicate to others what I had found to be the truth, the truth that would make me free, I had started to believe their stuff, their truth, which was that there is no truth, just many beliefs about what is true.

However, something within me said trust what you hear, not with your ears, but with your spirit. You had reached the conclusion that the Bible had the truth after studying other religions, occults, numerology and some astrology. Thus, from these studies you had learned the truth; the Holy Bible has the truth.

The next step I took was trying to defend the Bible. However, later I would realize that the defense offered was more a defense of myself than of the Word of God. Nevertheless, in my heart, which was feeding off my renewed mind, I knew the truth. I knew that if an Afro-American says Jesus was a black man, it doesn't change the truth that Jesus was a Jew. Furthermore, when some professor wrote a book and said his research showed all Afro-Americans were inferior to Caucasians, it didn't make the statement the truth. Yet, if I believed and accepted the belief that truth was in the eye of the beholder, that what one believed was the truth, I would have to also accept the black Jesus and the superiority of Caucasians as the truth.

Even though I wandered in my belief, as many young Christians would, I knew there had to be a way of understanding the truth about

THE TRUTH: (WHAT IS TRUTH? AND WHERE DO I FIND TRUTH? THE TRUTH THAT WILL MAKE ME FREE)

truth. I would continue to accept the Bible as holding the truth, but I would avoid discussions about the Word of God being the truth. However, there was something inside me that said there had to be a common explanation, which would aid me in helping myself and others to understand what is the truth and where to find it.

Then one day the answer came to me. Along with the answer came the understanding. The answer and understanding came as quickly as the Texas weather can change and as sudden as the light which replaces the darkness when a switch is moved. The enlightenment was probably equal to Edison's response to discovering the light bulb and Bell's response to inventing the telephone.

The understanding came during a discussion an ex-friend and I were having, although she wasn't an ex at the time. But, you'll come to understand why she soon became an ex. The discussion centered on her telling me one thing on a Monday and a different thing the following Wednesday about the same occurrence.

The previous Friday she and I had made plans to go to the movies on Saturday. On Saturday, I called her to confirm where and when we would meet for the movie. There was no answer, so I left a message on her answering machine to return my call. As the beginning of the movie approached, I called her again and left a second message. Well the movie time and Saturday itself came and went without a return of my call.

On Sunday, I woke without receiving a call from her. I became very concerned and called her again. You're right – no answer, only the answer machine, and yes, I left another message to return my call.

It was on Monday, after work, when I heard from her. She informed me that she was at the hospital the entire weekend – all Saturday and Sunday. Early Saturday morning, she received a call from her cousin that the cousin's son, who was severely asthmatic, had an asthma attack. So, she, the soon-to-be ex-friend, had spent the entire Saturday and Sunday at the hospital. She went on to say she didn't call me about the movies or emergency because she was so upset about the cousin's son's illness that she had to be sedated all Saturday and Sunday.

"THE" DIET FOR YOUR MIND TO HELP YOU FIND THE TRUTH THAT WILL SET YOU FREE

On Wednesday, while visiting my ex at her place, she requested that I hand her the telephone bill from the table. While I was retrieving the bill, I saw a pizza receipt with the past Saturday's date and time of delivery. The receipt also said she could get a free soda if she made another order within two weeks. When I asked her who had the pizza on Saturday night she said she had the pizza after returning from the hospital on Saturday night. She went on to say my phone call wasn't returned on Sunday because she awoke late and went to church. Of course, after church she returned to the hospital.

Finally, I began to explain to her that she had told me one thing on the Monday, over the telephone, and a different thing today, Wednesday. On Monday she had stated that she was at the hospital for all of Saturday and Sunday. Today, she was saying she returned home on Saturday night. Then on Monday, she had said she didn't call because she was at the hospital the entire weekend and was sedated. Today she was saying she did go home on Saturday night and that she went to church on Sunday and then returned to the hospital.

I told her, "Your statements are inconsistent. Therefore, you are not telling me the truth." The truth would not contain inconsistent statements; rather it would contain consistent statements.

Included in the definition of truth found in the dictionary is the statement that truth is conformity with facts. Since facts are consistent, the truth is consistent.

I went on to give her the example of the five extensions on the hand, which I mentioned above. However, this time I used it to show consistency and inconsistency. When a normal hand is held up, there will be five extensions. If I held my normal hand before you and said I had five extensions, and then you saw five extensions, you would say I was telling the truth. Why am I telling the truth? I am telling the truth because what I have shown – five extensions – is consistent with my words "I have holding up a hand with five extensions." However, if I withdraw my thumb and display only four extensions, yet tell you that I am displaying five extensions, I am not telling the truth. Why am I not telling the truth? The reason I am not telling the truth is because my spoken words are inconsistent with what I display. So, since the display is not consistent with my words, there is inconsistency and a lack of truth.

THE TRUTH: (WHAT IS TRUTH? AND WHERE DO I FIND TRUTH? THE TRUTH THAT WILL MAKE ME FREE)

In the midst of my excitement in response to the new enlightenment, I found another example. I said to her, "If I told you that I have on my feet two black shoes and you looked at my feet and saw two black shoes, you would say I was telling the truth. On the other hand, if I said that I had two shoes on my feet and you looked at my feet and saw one shoe, then you would say that I was not telling the truth. Since there is no consistency, there is no truth."

My enlightenment came with the bonus of words in The Manual that would further assist in understanding what is truth and where to find the truth. In The Manual, at Hebrews 13:8, is found another consistency.

"Jesus Christ the same yesterday, and today, and forever."

Now that I had come to recognize the truth as consistency, the above scripture had shown me where to seek the truth. If consistency is truth, and Jesus is the same yesterday, today and forever, He is consistency – He is truth. Furthermore, since Jesus is God in the flesh, then God is truth.

Sanctify them through thy truth: thy word is truth.

And for their sakes I sanctify myself, that they also might be sanctified through the truth. (St. John 17:17,19)

Yes, I discovered what truth is and where to find it. Needless to say, the truth was not found in my ex-friend. Nor would I search for the truth in an individual unless that individual could show me the way of the truth and the life. Jesus says He is the way the truth and the life. He says this in The Manual. This is the best stuff. It's stuff from The Manual, the manual to be given to each creation, for the care of the creation, by the creator.

"THE" DIET FOR YOUR MIND TO HELP YOU FIND THE TRUTH THAT WILL SET YOU FREE

THE BATTLE BETWEEN LIES AND THE TRUTH

I am sure that even a six year old who has an iota of common sense has learned that life is full of differences and opposites. The little one has heard you say, when he or she has placed a shoe on the right foot that should be placed on the left foot, that the shoe is on the wrong foot. "Dear, put this shoe," we say, pointing to the left shoe, "on the left foot." And while holding the other shoe, we tell the child to place this shoe on the right foot. This, along with other common occurrences, teaches the child that there are differences.

In the above situation, the parents have taught the child that there is a right and a left. When parents express approval and disapproval in an act performed by a child, they teach the child the lesson that there is a right and a wrong. The parents who have been born-again, will teach their children that The Manual, The Truth, has another that is different and opposed to the truth. The opposite of the truth is a lie.

> For you are the children of your father the devil and you love to do evil things he does. He was a murderer from the beginning and a hater of truth-there is not an iota of truth in him. When he lies, it is perfectly normal, for he is the father of liars. And so when I tell the truth, you naturally don't believe it. (St John 8:44-45 TLB)

Later we will explore in more detail the creation of man by God. We will go to the Garden of Eden, which was a perfect place where man would abide – a place of innocence and a place of truth.

Then as the world turned, in the days of Adam and Eve lives. They were yet young and restless, searching for tomorrow, following the guiding light, with perfect health and no need for a general hospital, because they were bold and beautiful. But they didn't follow a diet for the mind and ate the forbidden fruit. The Mackintosh had moved from the Gateway and found itself saying, "<u>I</u>'ve <u>B</u>een <u>M</u>urdered."

The Word says Eve ate first and gave also to Adam. When Adam ate the fruit, realizing that now all born after him would possess the contamination of disobedience and death, he said to Eve, "Look what you've done to all my children."

Yes, a lie tried to murder the truth. It was the lie told to Eve by the serpent, Satan, that she would not die, but become as a god, that caused the physical and spiritual death of Adam, Eve, you and I. However, truth did not die. Only humanity's recognition of the truth died. Now humanity must observe what is said and who is saying what. Humanity must find a diet of truth, which includes the observation that there is an opposite diet consisting of evil and lies.

This deception, this lie told to Adam and Eve, was done in Satan's effort to father children. Remember at this point in existence, only Adam and Eve existed, and they were God's children. God's children were children of light and truth. Later when we look deeper into the origin of evil, we'll see that Lucifer, the same character as Satan or the Devil, was an angel of light. However, because of his disobedience, and attempt to take over heaven, he and others who followed him were kicked out of heaven. Then, when God created mankind, he sought humans whom he could get to follow him, thereby creating his followers or children.

Thus, Lucifer would have followers, children to create his kingdom of lies and evil, and was looking for believers to inhabit his kingdom. This is why the above scripture at St John 8:44-45 says Satan is the father of lies.

So, we have the creation, man, created in truth, who became contaminated with lies and now is confused. Are you still asking why put your mind on a diet?

Lies are deceiving. Lies want you to see four extensions on one hand, whereas truth wants you to see five extensions. Deceptions and lies will have you see a bright shining red sports car, whereas the truth will have you see the smoke coming from the tail pipe of the bright shining red car. Lies would have you believe that you, and only you, should be considered in any endeavor, whereas truth will have you love your neighbor as yourself.

Lies will destroy, whereas truth will create. Lies will destroy trust in a person, even your mate, whereas truth encourages and is the cornerstone of trust and faith.

"THE" DIET FOR YOUR MIND TO HELP YOU FIND THE TRUTH THAT WILL SET YOU FREE

I'm reminded of a hunting experience I shared with my father. We went hunting for rabbits one fall afternoon. Upon arriving at the hunting location, immediately a rabbit jumped up from the bushes and ran to my left. I began to chase the rabbit. My father called to me, "Son, what are you doing?" I replied, "Chasing the rabbit, to kill him." My father said, "Son, you don't have to chase the rabbit. All you have to do is stay still. The rabbit will run around in a circle. So, if you remain still, he will come to you." Needless to say, my father was right and the rabbit was the meat dish later that evening.

Later in life, I heard the statement that a lie will travel faster and further than the truth. A little later, I learned that a lie, like the rabbit, may run faster and further, but truth will not have to chase the lie, only be there to be the truth. Thus, a mind diet of truth does not include jogging and running after lies, rather a standing, standing on the truth. This truth one should be dieting on is Jesus, the Word, the Son of God, standing as the same, yesterday, today and forever.

WISDOM KNOWLEDGE AND "HOLY" UNDERSTANDING

While reviewing The Manual, the Holy Bible, I found that the Holy Bible is divided into two testaments, an Old Testament and a New Testament. There are thirty-nine books in the Old Testament and twenty-seven books in the New Testament. Thus, the total number of books in the Holy Bible is sixty-six.

As an attorney, I can tell you that the word testament usually is found in reference to a person's "last will and testament." This testament, when used in conjunction with a will, is the written act by which a person determines the disposal of his or her property at death. Thus, the testament is to be followed to the letter and spirit of its contents. The last will and testament is to be followed without question. It is said to be the truth about the individual's intentions regarding the disposal of his or her property.

Well, I read in the first book of God's Old Testament that God created the world and the people in it. Furthermore, the creator, God, gave humankind dominion over the world. So, immediately I am led to the creator and creation. This brings into play the theory – no the fact – that the creator knows what is best for the creation.

I am further reminded of an expression I have heard. The expression is that the Bible can be perceived as:

B-ASIC **I**-NFORMATION **B**-EFORE **L**-EAVING **E**-ARTH

Thus, we arrive back to why I call the Holy Bible a manual. It is the manual that instructs an individual how to use his or her earthly life.

While reviewing the index and introduction of each of the sixty-six books I found that one of sixty-six had been identified as The Book of Divine Wisdom. This book is called Proverbs.

The introduction to the Book of Proverbs states the book is a collection of sententious sayings, which are divine wisdom applied to the earthly conditions of the people of God.[1]

Since I had become one of God's people – we'll discuss this later – I went to this book. Even though Proverbs is literally the twentieth (20th) book in the Holy Bible, I began at Proverbs because I was seeking to further understand the need for a mental diet and the truth that would make me free.

I knew that I was on the right track in my search for knowledge, wisdom and understanding when wisdom and understanding were mentioned in the second verse of the first chapter.

The introduction to the Book of Proverbs also states that Solomon wrote Proverbs. Solomon was one of King David's sons, and he would become a king of Israel himself. The story about King Solomon and his wisdom can be found in the first book of Kings. David, the father of Solomon, was dying. He appointed Solomon as his successor. Then the following occurred.

> The Lord appeared to him in a dream that night and told him to ask for anything he wanted, and it would be given to him! Solomon replied, "You were wonderfully kind to my father David because he was honest and true and faithful to you, and obeyed your commands. And you have continued your kindness to him by giving him a son to succeed him.
>
> O Lord my God, now you have made me the king instead of my father David, but I am as a little child who doesn't know his way around. And here I am among your chosen people, a nation so great that there are almost too many people to count!
>
> Give me an understanding mind so that I can govern your people well and know the difference between what is right and what is wrong. For who by himself is able to carry such a heavy responsibility?"
>
> The Lord was pleased with his reply and was glad that Solomon had asked for wisdom. So he replied, "Because you have asked for wisdom in governing my people, and haven't asked for a long life or riches for yourself, or the defeat of your enemies - yes, I'll give you what you asked for! I will give you a wiser mind than anyone else has ever had or ever will have!
>
> And I will also give you what you didn't ask for - riches and honor! And no one in all the world will be as rich and famous as you for the rest of your life!

WISDOM KNOWLEDGE AND "HOLY" UNDERSTANDING

And I will give you a long life if you follow me and obey my laws as your father did." Then Solomon woke up and realized it had been a dream. He returned to Jerusalem and went into the Tabernacle. As he stood before the Ark of the Covenant of the Lord, he sacrificed burnt offerings and peace offerings. Then he invited all of his officials to a great banquet.

Soon afterward two young prostitutes came to the king to have an argument settled. "Sir," one of them began, "We live in the same house, just the two of us, and recently I had a baby. When it was three days old, this woman's baby was born too. But her baby died during the night when she rolled over on it in her sleep and smothered it.

Then she got up in the night and took my son from beside me while I was asleep, and laid her dead child in my arms and took mine to sleep beside her. And in the morning when I tried to feed my baby it was dead! But when it became light outside, I saw that it wasn't my son at all."

Then the other woman interrupted, "It certainly was her son, and the living child is mine." And they argued back and forth before the king.

Then the king said, "Let's get the facts straight: both of you claim the living child, and each says that the dead child belongs to the other. All right bring me a sword." So a sword was brought to the king. Then he said, "Divide the living child in two and give half to each of these women!"

Then the woman who really was the mother of the child, and who loved him very much, cried out, "Oh, no, sir! Give her the child – don't kill him!" But the other woman said, "All right, it will be neither yours nor mine; divide it between us!"

Then the king said, "Give the baby to the woman who wants him to live, for she is the mother!"

"THE" DIET FOR YOUR MIND TO HELP YOU FIND THE TRUTH THAT WILL SET YOU FREE

> Word of the king's decision spread throughout the entire nation, and all the people were awed as they realized the great wisdom God had given him. (1 Kings 3:5-28 TLB)

The above is presented in support of my going to the Proverbs. Furthermore, the introduction states that chapters one through seven were written to his sons and chapters eight and nine were written in praise of wisdom.

Solomon, remember, is the person that God promised a wise and understanding heart, which would never be equaled. Thus, even without sound wisdom, it would behoove an individual to inquire of the best in the area where the individual was seeking guidance.

Solomon instructed his son to get wisdom and understanding.

> Get wisdom, get understanding: forget it not; neither decline from the words of my mouth. Wisdom is the principal thing; therefore get wisdom: and with all thy getting get understanding. (Proverbs 4: 5 and 6)

I reviewed the definition of wisdom, knowledge and understanding in the dictionary. The dictionary would say that wisdom is the quality of being wise and intelligence and of drawing on experience and being governed by prudence, a store of knowledge. Then knowledge is the state of knowing and understanding. To understand is to have the power of comprehension – to possess knowledge.

Through the wise words of the wisest man to live, I had come to the question, what should I understand? Then the wise one spoke:

THE FEAR OF THE LORD IS THE BEGINNING OF WISDOM: AND THE KNOWLEDGE OF THE HOLY IS UNDERSTANDING. (Proverbs 9:10)

Now I knew where to begin with wisdom and what I was to understand. Fear of God I would understand later to mean reverence for God. In other words, one must show honor or respect toward God, and trust God and respond with hatred of evil.

After being informed that the knowledge of the holy is understanding, I began to seek knowledge of the holy.

WISDOM KNOWLEDGE AND "HOLY" UNDERSTANDING

In Genesis, the book of beginnings, I found the beginning of heaven and earth. Furthermore, therein is found the beginning of mankind.

In the beginning God created the heaven and the earth. (Gen. 1:1)

And God said, let the earth bring forth the living creature after his kind, cattle, and creeping thing, and beast of the earth after his kind: and it was so. And God made the beast of the earth after his kind, and cattle after their kind, and everything that creepeth upon the earth after his kind: and God saw that it was good. And God said, Let us make man in our image, after our likeness: and let them have dominion over the fish of the sea, and over the foul of the air, and over the cattle, and over all the earth, and over every creeping thing that creepeth upon the earth. So God created man in his own image, in the image of God created he him: male and female created he them. (Gen 1:24-27)

And the Lord God formed man of the dust of the ground, and breathed into his nostrils the breath of life; and man became a living soul. Then the Lord planted a garden in Eden, to the east, and placed in the garden the man he had formed. (Gen 2:7-8)

The Lord God planted all sorts of beautiful trees there in the garden, trees producing the choicest of fruit. At the center of the garden he placed the Tree of Life, and also the Tree of Conscience, giving knowledge of Good and Bad. (Gen 2:8-9 TLB)

The Lord God placed the man in the Garden of Eden as its gardener, to tend and care for it. But the Lord God gave the man this warning: "You may eat any fruit in the garden except fruit from the Tree of Conscience – for its fruit will open your eyes to make you aware of right and wrong, good and bad. If you eat its fruit, you will be doomed to die. (Gen 2:15-17 TLB

"THE" DIET FOR YOUR MIND TO HELP YOU FIND THE TRUTH THAT WILL SET YOU FREE

>Now although the man and his wife were naked, neither of them was embarrassed or ashamed (Gen 2:25 TLB)
>
>The serpent was the craftiest of all the creatures the Lord God made. So the serpent came to the woman. "Really?" he asked. "None of the fruit in the garden? God says you mustn't eat any of it?"
>
>"Of course we may eat it," the woman told him. "It's only the fruit from the tree at the center of the garden that we are not to eat. God says we mustn't eat it or even touch it, or we will die."
>
>That's a lie!" the serpent hissed. "You'll not die! God knows very well that the instant you eat it you will become like him, for your eyes will be opened – you will be able to distinguish good from evil!" The woman was convinced. How lovely and fresh looking it was! And it would make her so wise! So she ate some of the fruit and gave some to her husband, and he ate it too. And as they ate it, suddenly they became aware of their nakedness, and were embarrassed. So they strung fig leaves together to cover themselves around the hips.
>
>Then the Lord said, "Now that the man has become as we are, knowing good from bad, what if he eats the fruit of the Tree of Life and lives forever?" So the Lord God banished him forever from the Garden of Eden, and sent him out to farm the ground from which he had been taken.
>
>Thus God expelled him, and placed mighty angels at the east of the Garden of Eden, with a flaming sword to guard the entrance to the Tree of Life. (Gen 3:1-7,and 22-24 TLB)

Did I not say that this was good stuff? Let's review the above that was stated in Genesis.

Genesis says that God created the heavens, the earth, the plants, animals and human life.

WISDOM KNOWLEDGE AND "HOLY" UNDERSTANDING

When the Lord God decided to make man he said, "Let us make man in our image, after our likeness:" So he created male and female.

Then man was given a home in a garden. He was instructed not to eat of the Tree of Good and Evil, the Tree of Conscience. Thus, he was originally created to walk in the Spirit. However, his eating of the forbidden fruit, which opened his eyes to nakedness, was evidence that he had come to know the physical and he had fallen from pure spirit to knowledge of the physical and spirit. Also, mankind was sentenced to death. Later, I would understand that not only would there be a physical death – the death of physical life, or of the body – but there would also be a spiritual death caused by the eating of the forbidden fruit - a separation of man from God, the Spirit.

The separation of mankind from God, the Spirit, caused a separation of mankind from the Tree of Life. So, there would be a need for a reconciling and a new birth. Adam and Eve were expelled from the garden.

"THE" DIET FOR YOUR MIND TO HELP YOU FIND THE TRUTH THAT WILL SET YOU FREE

IN THE IMAGE AND LIKENESS OF GOD

> And God said, Let us make man in our image, after our likeness: and let him have dominion over the fish of the sea, and over the fowl of the air, ...(Genesis 1:26)

There have been many opinions on what is meant about man being made in the image of God. One of these opinions says that the above scripture is saying that we, mankind, look like God. Thereby, concluding that God is a physical being. However, I have found in the Manual, a scripture that would refute that position or belief.

> God is a spirit: and they that worship him must worship him in spirit and truth. (St. John 4:24)

Then there is the part that states, "After our likeness:" What does "our likeness" mean? Could the Living Bible's paraphrase explain the likeness?

> Then God said, "Let us make man – someone like ourselves, to be the master of all life upon the earth and in the skies and in the seas." So God made man like his master. Like God did God make man. Man and maid did he make them. (Gen 1:26-27 TLB)

This is the answer. There is additional proof that the "likeness to God" found in mankind conveys the dominion of mankind over all creatures in, on and above the earth. Adam's dominion over the earth can be found in God allowing Adam to name the creatures created in, on and above the earth.

> So the Lord God formed from the soil every kind of animal and bird, and brought them to the man to see what he would call them; and whatever he called them, that was their name . . . . . (Gen 2:19-20 TLB)

Man's being created in the "image and likeness of God" is fully substantiated in man's having dominion over the earth.

Then there is another "image and likeness of God" found in mankind. As an image, a reproduction or imitation of a person or thing, or a mental picture of something not actually present, man was given the ability to create, just like God.

IN THE IMAGE AND LIKENESS OF GOD

However, to better understand and to get wisdom and holy understanding in the search for the truth, I had to understand who the "us," "we" and "our" were in the above scripture. All of these pronouns are plural. Thus, they had to represent more than one being. The question may be asked, why is this – the plural pronoun – important? Well, remember Proverbs said the knowledge of the Holy is understanding.

Understanding of the "we," "us" and "our" has led to the spiritual confirmation of the Tri-God existence. When God said "let us," he was speaking to the Son, Jesus, and the Holy Spirit. The Tri-God is often referred to as the Holy Trinity; it has three parts. So, the Tri-God or Holy Trinity consists of God the Father, God the Son, and God the Holy Spirit.

> But when the comforter is come, whom I will send unto you from the Father, even the Spirit of truth, which proceedeth from the Father, he shall testify of me; (St John 15:26)

There are numerous scriptures I could quote to substantiate the Tri-God existence. As we travel on in search for the truth that will make us free, we will find other scriptures that support some other position, but these also support the Tri-God existence.

The Tri-God is God the Father, known as Jehovah, God the Son, known as Jesus the Christ, and God the Holy Spirit, called sometimes the Comforter. There is one God, but this one God has three personalities. Furthermore, each of these personalities exists for a specific purpose.

Now if you are still physically bonded, trying to understand how one can be three and three can be one, then let us turn to the physical. God has always given a physical representation of the spiritual existence.

Let's say you are a female, married with children. Then, to your children you are a mother. To your husband you are a wife, and to your parents you are a child.

If you are a male married with children, the following are the ways you may be addressed. Your parents call you a child. Your wife refers to you as the husband. The children will call you Dad, Father.

"THE" DIET FOR YOUR MIND TO HELP YOU FIND THE TRUTH THAT WILL SET YOU FREE

In each example above, there is one person who has three points of reference. Furthermore, each reference causes a difference in personality or acts performed. The husband looks upon his wife as being a part of himself. The son must honor and obey his parents. A father must grow the gifts of God given and entrusted to him. Thus we have the one male who has three purposes – one who is three.

This is the way we need to view the Tri-God: the one God with his three existences. We must view the spiritual existence of the Tri-God as "us" in the "Let us make man."

Within the sixty-six books, the responsibility of each in the Tri-God's existences can be found. The following is offered for visualization.

GOD	**RESPONSIBILITY**
God the Father	Power, Courage, and Strength
God the Son	Creation, Life and Love
God the Holy Spirit	Wisdom, Knowledge and The Truth

THE TRINITY OF GOD: THE FATHER, SON, AND HOLY SPIRIT

FIRST PERSON
(GOD THE FATHER)

When we think of an earthly, physical, father, we are looking at a parent who is considered to be the strength of the home. Thus, when we consider the Heavenly Father, the Spiritual Father, we are also led to find in this personality strength. Along with his strength, we find courage and power.

In an effort to be politically correct, but not spiritually incorrect, I risk saying that when there is one parent, male or female, with God as the Spiritual Father of that house, he allows the male or female to be the "Father" – the strength, power and courage of that house.

However, in the so-called norm, it is the father, a male, whom God has placed over the family to protect the family. To protect the family, the father must be strong in adversity. The father must have the strength to endure all circumstances. The power, as we will see later, has to come from his, the father's, the Heavenly Father's power.

The review or overview of the first thirty-nine books, The Old Testament of The Holy Bible, shows the power, courage and strength of God the Father. The father's power was used to destroy Sodom and Gomorrah. We have seen His courage in trusting man after the eating of the forbidden fruit and the coming of so much evil that God had to destroy the world. Then we have seen his strength in protecting his children: he protected Daniel in the lions' den and he protected the Israelite boys when they were facing the fire in the fiery furnace.

Even Jesus recognized the responsibility and personality of an earthly father and compared him to the Heavenly Father.

> Ask, and you will be given what you ask for. Seek, and you will find. Knock, and the door will open. For everyone who asks, receives. Anyone who seeks, finds. If only you will knock, the door will open. If a child asks his father for a loaf of bread, will he be given a stone instead? If he asks for fish, will he be given a

poisonous snake? Of course not! And if you hardhearted, sinful men know how to give good gifts to your children, won't your father in heaven even more certainly give good gifts to those who ask him for them? (St. Matthew 7:7-11 TLB)

SECOND PERSON
(GOD THE SON, JESUS)

One of the reasons I appreciate the New Testament is the coming of God the Father to the earth as God the Son. In God the Father, we find God relating to man from the outside. God in the personality of Jesus began the restoration of the personal relationship between mankind and God from the inside. As the Father, He wrote His desires for mankind on stone. These desires are written as the Ten Commandments. However, God as the Son made it possible to write his desires in the heart and mind of mankind.

For finding fault with them, he saith, Behold, the days come, saith the Lord, when I will make a new covenant with the house of Israel and with the house of Judah:

For this is the covenant that I will make with the house of Israel after those days, saith the Lord; I will put my laws into their mind, and write them in their hearts: and I will be to them a God, and they shall be to me a people:

And they shall not teach every man his neighbor, and every man his brother, saying, Know the Lord: for all shall know me, from the least to the greatest. (Hebrews 8:8,10-11)

There may be some concern that the above states the covenant was only made with the nation of Israel. Let's read a little further.

Is he the God of Jews only? Is he not also of the Gentiles? Yes, of the Gentiles also: (Romans 3:29)

For ye are all the children of God by faith in Christ Jesus. There is neither Jew nor Greek, there is neither bond nor free, there is neither male nor female: for ye are one in Christ Jesus. And if ye be Christ's, then are ye Abraham's seed, and heirs according to the promise. (Galatians 3:26, 28-29)

The Old Testament of the Holy Bible, the revealing of God the Father, would be like the Torah. Thus, the laws were given to the Jewish nation as God's chosen people. They were chosen people that other races and nationalities would observe to see the One God. This would cause other nations to want to be like Mike – I'm sorry – to be like the Jews. The chosen people, the Jews, would live as an example of a people who had The Father's blessings.

The New Testament shows God taking on flesh and entering this world. It shows the Son coming to offer reconciliation and to re-establish the personal relationship between the Heavenly Father and humanity. Remember that the personal relationship was lost in the Garden of Eden. This reconciling would again be by an inward relationship as opposed to an outward one. The system, which would identify this "new" relationship would be called love.

For God so loved the world that he gave his only begotten Son, that whosoever believeth in him should not perish, but have everlasting life. (St John 3:16)

I will speak on love later. An entire chapter will be utilized to get knowledge of the "holy love," thereby bringing understanding in our search for the truth that will make us free. The purpose here is to show the three personalities at work.

THIRD PERSON
(GOD THE HOLY SPIRIT)

And I will pray the Father, and he shall give you another Comforter, that he may bide with you for ever; Even the Spirit of truth; whom the world cannot receive, because it seeth him not, neither knoweth him: but ye know him; for he dwelleth with you, and shall be in you. (St. John 14:16-17)

Howbeit when he, the Spirit of truth, is come, he will guide you into all truth: for he shall not speak of

> himself; but whatsoever he shall hear, that will he speak; and he will shew you things to come. (St. John 16:13)
>
> And the Spirit of the Lord shall rest upon him, the Spirit of wisdom, understanding, counsel and might; the Spirit of knowledge and of the fear of the Lord. His delight will be obedience to the Lord. He will not judge by appearance, false evidence, or hearsay, but will defend the poor and the exploited. He will rule against the wicked who oppress them. For he will be clothed with fairness and with truth. (Isaiah 11:2-5 TLB)

In the personality of God the Holy Spirit, God is seeking to bring humanity back to God by enabling man to understand God's understanding. Thus, if there is a human understanding and a Holy understanding and a change from human to Godly (spiritual) understanding, there must be a change in man. This change must be through a new birth, which will lead to a new mind. The new or renewed mind will not have a human source, but a spiritual one.

> So shalt thou find favor and good understanding in the sight of God and man. Trust in the Lord with all thine heart; and lean not unto thine own understanding. In all thy ways acknowledge him, and he shall direct thy paths. (Proverbs 3:4-6)

Or, as presented in The Living Bible at Proverbs 3:4-6:

> If you want favor with both God and man, and a reputation for good judgment and common sense, then trust the Lord completely; don't ever trust yourself. In everything you do, put God first, and he will direct you and crown your effort with success.

We have already seen that understanding comes by wisdom and knowledge. After all, the realization of the need for understanding humanity's purpose on earth has led us to realize that we need spiritual wisdom and knowledge. Thus, after getting wisdom and knowledge, we obtain understanding. Then, after understanding is completed, we are automatically in the truth, the truth that will set us free.

THE TRINITY OF GOD: THE FATHER, SON, AND HOLY SPIRIT

In the Holy Spirit giving wisdom, knowledge and truth is also the ability to help humanity, or should I say help Christians, when a person doesn't have the wisdom and knowledge in search for truth.

> Likewise the Spirit also helpeth our infirmities: for
> we know not what we should pray for as we ought: but
> the Spirit itself maketh intercession for us with
> groanings which cannot be uttered. (Romans 8:26)

However, at this point of discussion, we are just recognizing that the One True God has three personalities. Each of these personalities exists for the purpose of God's creation – man and woman. Each of these personalities will be further developed later. Suffice it to say that there is a reason for the Tri-God. The understanding that man and woman are made in the "likeness and image" of God leads us to the understanding that man has a tri-person existence.

"THE" DIET FOR YOUR MIND TO HELP YOU FIND THE TRUTH THAT WILL SET YOU FREE

TWO DISPENSATIONS
(INNOCENCE AND CONSCIENCE)

I hope you haven't forgotten the scripture found in Genesis stated above, where it is stated that man was formed from the earth, received the breath of life in his nostrils and became a living soul. Man was given instructions what to do. One instruction was not to eat of the Tree of Knowledge of good and evil. When God gives a specific revelation of his will, man is tested for his obedience to the same. This period of time is called a dispensation. There are seven such dispensations, which are distinguished in the Manual.

The first dispensation is **INNOCENCY.** Man was created innocent, placed in a perfect environment, subjected to an absolutely simple test, and warned of the consequence of disobedience. The dispensation of innocence ended in the judgment of the Expulsion. The above scripture at Genesis 3:24, which states that man and woman were removed from the garden, refers to the Expulsion.

The next, or second dispensation is **CONSCIENCE.** The disobedient man came to a personal and experimental knowledge of good and evil – of good as obedience and evil as disobedience to the known will of God. So, through that knowledge conscience was awakened. In other words, God created man as uncontaminated (innocent). It could be said that man was purely a spiritual being, a living soul with only God to follow. But, when contamination came (eating the forbidden fruit), there was a change. Now man could not only obey God, his creator, but also be aware of the physical that allowed a choice – a choice between the instructions of God the Spirit and physical impulses.

These two dispensations are mentioned, so when later the call to be born again is put forth, the call will be rational even to the physical mind.

In summary, we could state the following: God the Father, Son, and Holy Spirit created man as a spirit, with a body and soul. In his disobedience, man left his original state of spirit (innocence) and his conscience was awakened. The awakening of the conscience brought change to man's spirit, body and soul. Now he had God-consciousness, world-consciousness and self-consciousness. Let's visualize this.

FATHER	**SON**	**HOLY SPIRIT**
THE SPIRIT	THE BODY	THE SOUL
(THE MIND)	(THE PHYSICAL)	(THE HEART)
GOD-consciousness	*World-consciousness*	*Self-consciousness*
(The will of God)	(The five senses)	(The emotions)

"THE" DIET FOR YOUR MIND TO HELP YOU FIND THE TRUTH THAT WILL SET YOU FREE

THE TRINITY OF HUMANITY
1. MAN AS A SPIRIT

The Manual has said that man was formed from dust and given a physical body. Then he received the breath of life via his nostrils and was given the Spirit of God. Thus he became a living soul, a being with individual and independent existence.

But God hath revealed them unto us by his Spirit: for the Spirit searcheth all things, yea, the deep things of God. For what man knoweth the things of a man, save the spirit of man which is in him? Even so the things of God knoweth no man, but the Spirit of God. Now we have received, not the spirit of the world, but the spirit which is of God; that we might know the things that are freely given to us of God. (1 Corinthians 2: 10-12)

I believe that man is a spirit, or has the spirit of God inside of him because the Spirit was breathed into his nostrils. Furthermore, the scripture above states that the Spirit of God lives inside of the children of God. The spirit is that part of man which is his mind. The mind of man is where man knows of God and is capable of God-consciousness, because he is allied to the spiritual creation.

This brings us to the necessity of being born again, which will be discussed later. Here the objective is to show that the root of man is the spirit.

2. MAN AS THE BODY

The body of a person is the only physical part of the person. Thus, the body is subject to death. However, the body serves as the seat of the senses, the means by which the spirit and soul have world-consciousness. In other words, man was given a physical body to carry the Spirit of God and a soul that would live even after the physical body died.

3. MAN AS THE SOUL

The soul of a person is where the affections, desires, the emotions, and active will – the self of a person – is found. So, a person is an individual, a self. Since a person is a self, he or she has self-consciousness.

When an attempt is made to define "soul," the definition cannot be a concrete one. The dictionaries would say that the soul is a spiritual and moral force – a person's total self, a spiritual principal embodied in human beings. When the understanding of the soul and spirit as stated above is completed, then one will see and embrace the differences.

In The Manual, there are references in the Old and New Testaments to the soul. In summary I have concluded that when God made man he made man two-part spirit and one-part physical. After the physical body dies, the soul and spirit live on. Let us not forget that the "soul" became contaminated when the forbidden fruit was eaten. Thus, it is not this physical body that will live on and on. Rather, the soul, the self-existence will live after the physical body is dead. When The Manual mentions a soul that dies, it refers to a soul that is not saved, that will not come to peace when absent from the body. The unsaved soul, which lives, will live in torment. Thus, we come to the wisdom, knowledge and understanding that man and woman were created physically and were not to physically die. But the scripture said Adam's eating of the forbidden fruit brought death.

Note there were three deaths: death of the spirit, the separation of man from God; death of the physical body – from dust it was made and to dust it will return; and death of the soul – the eternal separation of man from God.

We must now come to understand the difference in what is called death. The dictionary defines death as a permanent cessation of all vital functions: the end of life, the passing or destruction of something inanimate.

The dictionary has assisted our understanding of physical and spiritual death. The body's death will appear in the physical returning of dust to dust, or the tangible to the tangible. There will be a readily identifiable cessation of life. However, spiritual death will appear in

"THE" DIET FOR YOUR MIND TO HELP YOU FIND THE TRUTH THAT WILL SET YOU FREE

the spiritual, as an intangible separation from an intangible spirit. In the case of the death of the spirit and death of the soul, there is a separation of man from God, or we could say, the destruction of an intimate relationship.

The physical body's death is readily identifiable. However, a spiritual death or death of the soul is not readily recognizable from the physical perspective. But, the spiritual manual will explain that which is spirit.

> Don't be afraid of those who can kill only the bodies – but can't touch your soul! Fear only God who can destroy both soul and body in hell. (St. Matthew 10:28 TLB)
>
> What profit is there if you gain the whole world – and lose eternal life? What can be compared with the value of eternal life? (St. Matthew 16:26 TLB)
>
> For what is a man profited, if he shall gain the whole world, and lose his soul? or what shall a man give in exchange for his soul? (St. Matthew 16:26)

The above scriptures at Matthew 16:26 show us that the soul will live eternally after the body dies. However, when God created the person, he intended, by giving the person a self-existence, to create a part of man that was always like God, which God could guide, and to whom He could be a Father. However, when the forbidden fruit was eaten, the soul became endowed with a good spirit, which was of God, and a bad spirit, which was of self. The self could make a decision to be obedient or disobedient to the Spirit that gave self its life.

Often the "heart" is used synonymously with the soul. The heart here is not the physical heart that can be located in the physical body. Remember that only the body is the physical part of the tri-person – a person with three existences. The heart that is synonymous with the soul is a spiritual heart. Thus, it cannot be seen as with the spirit.

God the Son, Jesus, taught the difference between the human physical heart and the spiritual heart, the soul. The Pharisees and other Jewish leaders criticized Jesus' disciples for disobeying the Jewish ritual of ceremonial hand-washing before they ate. Jesus, who had come to earth to teach the spiritual, responded with this reply:

THE TRINITY OF HUMANITY

This people draweth nigh unto me with their mouth, and honoureth me with their lips; but their heart is far from me.

Not that which goeth into the mouth defileth a man; but that which cometh out of the mouth, this defileth a man.

Do not ye yet understand, that whatsoever entereth in at the mouth goeth into the belly, and is cast out into the draught? But those things which proceed out of the mouth come forth from the heart: and they defile the man. For out of the heart proceed evil thoughts, murders, adulteries, fornications, thefts, false witness, blasphemies: These are the things which defile a man: but to eat with unwashen hands defileth not a man. (St. Matthew 15:8,11, 17-20).

You aren't made unholy by eating non-Kosher food! It is what you say and think that makes you unclean.

Don't you see that anything you eat passes through the digestive tract and out again? But evil words come from an evil heart, and defile the man who says them. (St. Matthew 15:11,18 TLB)

Now we have the wisdom and knowledge that the Manual's "heart" refers to a spiritual heart, a heart that can't be seen by the physical eye. This heart has to do with desires. It is rooted in what the spirit of good says or what the spirit of evil says. It deals in the thoughts, desires, and total emotions of a person, whether good, coming from the Spirit of God, or evil, coming from the spirit of evil.

"THE" DIET FOR YOUR MIND TO HELP YOU FIND THE TRUTH THAT WILL SET YOU FREE

A SOUL TO BE SAVED

It has been mentioned that the purpose of this physical existence is to prepare for a spiritual existence. Furthermore, the physical body will not be saved.

> "In the sweat of thy face shalt thou eat bread, till thou return unto the ground; for out of it wast thou taken; for dust thou art, and unto dust shalt thou return." (Genesis 3:19)

However, there is a spiritual body, which includes a spiritual heart that will be saved.

> Death came into the world because of what one man (Adam) did, and it is because of what this other man (Christ) has done that now there is the resurrection from the dead. Everyone dies because all of us are related to Adam, being members of his sinful race, and wherever there is sin, death results. But all who are related to Christ will rise again. Each, however, in his own turn: Christ rose first; then when Christ comes back, all his people will become alive again.
>
> But someone may ask, "How will the dead be brought back to life again? What kind of bodies will they have?" What a foolish question! You will find the answer in your own garden! When you put a seed into the ground it doesn't grow into a plant unless it "dies" first. And when the green shoot comes up out of the seed, it is very different from the seed you first planted . . .
>
> In the same way, our earthly bodies which die and decay are different from the bodies we shall have when we come back to life again, for they will never die. The bodies we have now embarrass us for they become sick and die; but they will be full of glory when we come back to life again. Yes, they are weak, dying bodies now, but when we live again they will be full of

strength. They are just human bodies at death, but when they come back to life they will be superhuman bodies. For just as there are natural, human bodies, there are also supernatural, spiritual bodies.

The scripture tell us that the first man, Adam, was given a natural, human body but Christ is more than that, for he was life-giving spirit.

First, then, we have these human bodies and later on God gives us spiritual, heavenly bodies. Adam was made from the dust of the earth, but Christ came from heaven above. Every human being has a body like Adam's, made of dust, but all who become Christ's will have the same kind of body as his – a body from heaven. Just as each of us now has a body like Adam's, so we shall some day have a body like Christ's.

I tell you this, my brothers: an earthly body cannot get into God's kingdom. These perishable bodies of ours are not the right kind to live forever. But I am telling you this strange and wonderful secret: we shall not all die, but we shall all be given new bodies! It will all happen in a moment, in the twinkling of an eye, when the last trumpet blast is blown. For there will be a trumpet blast from the sky and all the Christians who have died will suddenly become alive, with new bodies that will never, never die: and then we who are still alive shall suddenly have new bodies too. For our earthly bodies, the ones we have now that can die, must be transformed into heavenly bodies that cannot perish but will live forever. (I Corinthians 15:21-23, 35-37, 42-53 TLB)

All the above is saying there is a physical and there is a spiritual existence. As the present finds human beings with a spirit, body and soul, the new, spiritual heavenly being will have a spirit body and soul. The physical body will die. The heavenly body will live on. So, in the human, natural body, or heavenly body there is a soul. The soul is where we find eternal life. Remember above we said, what would it profit a man to gain the whole world and lose his soul? Or, what

"THE" DIET FOR YOUR MIND TO HELP YOU FIND THE TRUTH THAT WILL SET YOU FREE

would it profit a man to gain in this physical world that which is temporal and live eternal life in torment?

To save a soul is to save the eternal existence of a soul from being separated from God the Spirit. But how did the soul get separated from God? The soul, the emotions, desires and affections of humanity were separated through sin.

SIN AND SINS

Most Theologians would define sin as knowingly or unknowing disobedience to the will of God. Sin originated with Satan and entered the world through Adam. Adam was told not to eat of the forbidden fruit, but ate anyway. This was disobedience to God. This is the type of act that is sin.

The first sin worked mortal ruin of the human race. Sin became a part of every human nature from Adam until today. This universal moral ruin is inherited from Adam.

Then there are acts, which are manifestations of sin, which are called "sins." In other words, because of what Adam did, and because Adam was the first of creation, then "sin" or Adam's nature is in each person when he or she is born. This sin or this nature of Adam will produce "sins."

I have seen the results of sin. The result of an act of sin is separation. In other words, the result of sin is:

S - EPARATION, **I** – SOLATION, **N** – EUTRALIZATION.

A quick review and analytical approach of the first disobedience to the will of God will show the above results.

Before eating the forbidden fruit, Adam and Eve would meet and visit with God. I am reminded here of God meeting with Adam to have Adam name the animals. However, once the fruit was eaten, the scripture says they hid themselves. Thus, instead of wanting to be close to God, their creator, Adam and Eve no longer had the feeling of acceptance; rather they had a conscience of their own and went to the next step, which is isolation.

In isolation, they wanted to be away from their creator. As with any violator of a known law, they sought to separate and isolate themselves from God, who gave the law, by hiding.

When the creation (creature) is separated and isolated from the creator, there is a lack of knowing. Consequently where there is a lack of knowledge, wisdom and understanding, the creature cannot

"THE" DIET FOR YOUR MIND TO HELP YOU FIND THE TRUTH THAT WILL SET YOU FREE

exercise any power given by the creator. Thus, the creation is neutralized. It has no power, courage or strength.

When we, who have been born-again, commit sins, we could say:

S – AINTS **I** – N **N** – EUTRAL **S** – ERVICE

> Knowing this, that our old man is crucified with him, that the body of sin might be destroyed, that henceforth we should not serve sin. (Romans 6:6)
>
> No man can serve two masters: for either he will hate the one, and love the other: or else he will hold to the one, and despise the other. Ye cannot serve God and mammon. (St Matthew 6:24)

Saints is another name given to the followers of Christ. Often Paul in his Epistles (Letters) to the churches would identify himself and or the members of a church as saints.

> Unto the church of God which is at Corinth, to them that are sanctified in Christ Jesus, called to be saints, with all that in every place call upon the name of Jesus Christ our Lord, both their's and our's: (I Corinthians 1:2)

So, a "Saint In Neutral Service" (SINS) will not be in the position of power or service. After all, the saint's main responsibility is to serve God. This serving God is partially accomplished by serving fellow humanity.

> After that he poureth water into a bason, and began to wash the disciples' feet, and to wipe them with the towel wherewith he was girded.
>
> So after he had washed their feet, and had taken his garments, and was set down again, he said to them, Know ye what I have done to you? Ye call me Master and Lord: and ye say well; for so I am. If I then, your Lord and Master, have washed your feet; ye also ought to wash one another's feet. For I have given you an example, that ye should do as I have done to you. (St. John 13:5, 12-15)

> Not with eyeservice, as men-pleasers; but as the servants of Christ, doing the will of God from the heart; With good will doing service, as the Lord, and not to men. (Ephesians 6:6-7)

We serve others by and through Christ. So being without Christ, or being disconnected from Christ, will leave a saint as the disconnected cable car. The cable car cannot remain in motion, which is its main function. So, if the cable is disconnected from the electrical power source, it will become motionless. Thus, the cable car is in neutral.

So, sins in the saint will bring saints in neutral service. Then the saint is in a similar position to the person who has not been born again – separated, isolated and neutralized. However, the saints, contrary to the belief of some, don't have to be born again because of committing a sin, but only have to confess the sin and return to the position of being able to serve God. (See I John 1:9)

Now the person who hasn't been born again will just remain separated, isolated and neutralized. The separation from God leads to service that is not from God. The sin produces sins and the person becomes sin. So rather than give to humanity, selfishness says to receive all you can. The service, if any, to humanity is for some quid pro quo (something for something). Thus sinners' service serves mammon, not God.

When we, who have been reconciled to God through Christ Jesus, can share the definition and result of sin as a separation, isolation and neutralization from our creator, rather than because sin is the work of Satan, then we'll find more souls that will be saved. The reason this is suggested is that most of us don't know who Satan is. Furthermore, hell and brimstones are of another world. However, the understanding of being separated from the creator, whether the physical creator, our earthly parents, or the spiritual creator, God, can be understood in the now.

WHO IS SATAN?

Before we attempt to understand who Satan is, we need to realize a truth, a truth, which is arrived at by holy understanding. This truth is that just as the God of the good has three existences, so does the god of evil. As with the God of the good, each part of the god of evil has an assigned task. Like good forces, evil forces have interchangeable abilities. Thus, the evildoer may be called Satan in one instance but the personality of the Devil may also be present. In short, there is one father of evil, but three personalities. As the good has three personalities while being one, so does the evil. And as it is wise to know the good, it is even wiser to know the bad. For if you have not aligned yourself with the good, you can rest assured that when and if you do align with the good, the evil will introduce itself.

Furthermore, doesn't it make spiritual sense that if the good is to be known as one but three, then evil will also be present as three, in order to work against the good?

THE TRINITY OF EVIL:
LUCIFER, SATAN, AND THE DEVIL

Lucifer	Satan	Devil
The father of evil	The prince of this world	Seeks souls
(Primary work done: in the spirit)	(Primary work done: thru the physical)	(Primary work done: in emotions, heart)
Mind	Body	Soul

FIRST PERSON
(LUCIFER)

As Lucifer, evil is most personified. There is not much known of the genesis of Lucifer other than what theologians have concluded from spiritual wisdom, knowledge, truth and holy understanding. The great theologian, The Reverend C. I. Scofield,[1] says Lucifer was apparently created as one of the Cherubim. The Cherubims are living creatures, actual beings of the angelic order, which has to do with the holiness of God. We shouldn't forget that the Lord placed Cherubims to prevent access to the Tree of Life.

> How you are fallen from heaven, O Lucifer, son of the morning! How you are cut down to the ground – mighty though you were against the nations of the world. For you said to yourself, "I will ascend to heaven and rule the angels. I will take the highest throne. I will preside on the Mount of Assembly far away in the north. I will climb to the highest heavens and be like the Most High." But instead, you will be brought down to the pit of hell, down to its lowest depths. (Isaiah 14:12-15 TLB)

The above information reveals the origin of the opposite of good, evil. Therein also is the author of evil identified. Lucifer, an angel of high authority and responsibility became prideful and was expelled from heaven. Furthermore, not only was Lucifer kicked out, but other angels, who aligned themselves with Lucifer's position of pride and disobedience, were kicked out also.

Yes, God kicked him out, but God being a just God, allowed Lucifer to live. How can one reach the conclusion that Lucifer lived? Furthermore, why is Lucifer considered to be working in the spiritual world, if God kicked him out?

To find an answer that is consistent with the truth, we must consider the word known in the religious community as excommunication.

Excommunication is defined in Webster's as an ecclesiastical censure, depriving a person of the rights of church membership, exclusion from fellowship in a group or community.

The above definition gives us an understanding that the phrase "kicked out" refers to an exclusion of fellowship. Lucifer was cherubim, one who had continuous fellowship with God the Father, but was removed from this constant presence due to pride. Then the conclusion is reached in The Manual that he was kicked out, removed from the continuous presence of God. Then he not only still lived, but lived in the spiritual world.

SECOND PERSON
(SATAN)

Before we move further we have to recognize a truth. That is that when evil appears before God about the physical earth, it appears as Satan, the prince of the physical world. Also, we must remember that the names Lucifer, Satan, and Devil all refer to the same creature. The names are given to identify or recognize the function of evil. Thus, as stated above, Satan is the name given for operations in the physical.

Therefore, in his spiritual position he still has access to God. How can I naturally explain this? It's like having a dog, which is a house pet. That cherished living creature will make the fatal mistake of staining and odorizing your carpet. This occurred after you had informed him of the rule: thou shall not release thyself while in the house and upon the carpet. So, Fido was disobedient. You remove Fido from the house. Now, Fido has access to the house, but not continuous access to live in the house. So each morning, each day, twenty-four seven, and three hundred and sixty five days a year, Fido appears at the door for something. Fido will come accusing you of

THE TRINITY OF EVIL: LUCIFER, SATAN, AND THE DEVIL

treating the cat, Ms. Meow, better than him. He comes and says that the cat was on the couch while you were gone. Fido is always telling on the bird, who flew out of her cage. The hamster didn't run in his cage, as he should. This is going on and on: Fido wants to accuse others of disobedience because he has been convicted and evicted for his disobedience.

Since Lucifer had been kicked out of his original sphere, he had to find another place to seek to be the ruler. Thus, he looked to the new creation, the earth, and all that dwelled therein, which included man. Lucifer as Satan would through the earth and air try to establish a kingdom on earth, wherein he would become the prince of the same. Note, he wants to be king of the earth, but he didn't create the earth, so he can never be king as long as King Tri-God is living, and we know that the Tri-God will live to eternity. Anyway, God the Father is a spiritual being, and so is Lucifer. God the Father sent his son to earth to bring the inhabitants, humanity, back to God. Lucifer, as Satan, is here on earth trying to prevent the return.

The above example of Fido is an illustration of what's happening in heaven, the spiritual world.

>One day as the angels came to present themselves before the Lord, Satan, the Accuser, came with them.
>
>"Where have you come from?" the Lord asked Satan.
>
>And Satan replied, "From patrolling the earth."
>
>Then the Lord asked Satan, "Have you noticed my servant Job? He is the finest man in all the earth – a good man who fears God and will have nothing to do with evil."
>
>"Why shouldn't he, when you pay him so well?" Satan scoffed. "You have always protected him and his home and his property from all harm. You have prospered everything he does – look how rich he is! No wonder he 'worships' you! But just take away his wealth, and you'll see him curse you to your face!"
>
>(Job 1:6-11 TLB)

If you are not familiar with the Book of Job in the Manual, please acquaint yourself. The conclusion was that God allowed Satan to cause illness to Job, death to Job's children, and a lost of his earthly wealth. However, Job remained loyal to God and his health was returned and he was blessed seven fold in land animals and children. However, when you read the entire story you'll find Satan doing all that he could to get Job to turn away from God. This is his job as the prince of the power of the air, the spirit that now works in the children of disobedience. His job is to try to prevent humanity from knowing the truth that will set humanity free. Satan does this by tempting or leading a person to do wrong and then accusing the person before God of the wrongness.

THIRD PERSON
(THE DEVIL)

There was a famous comedian performing in the seventies and eighties whose punch line was, "The Devil made me do it!"

> He that committeth sin is of the devil; for the devil sinneth from the beginning . . . . (1 John 3:8)

> And supper being ended, the devil having now put into the heart of Judas Iscariot, Simon's son, to betray him: (St. John 13:2)

Above we have said that the Devil's primary work is done in the emotions, heart or soul. Thus, he seeks the soul by entering the mind with the thoughts of evil. It is the Devil at work when in the Manual Paul mentions that there is something that is at war with his mind. It is telling him to do wrong when he's trying to do right.

We have learned that when the heart in the spiritual sense is mentioned that the soul could be used as a synonym. Furthermore, the spiritual, the soul, is where all desires and affections and all of the self exist. Thus, the devil will enter the desires of a person, the person who is worldly alive but spiritually dead. So, when the desires which are of the liar, the sinner from the beginning, are passed through the senses of the world into a mind not on a diet, the devil is able to lead a person to the prophetic doom of hell.

> And they arrived at the country of the Gadarenes, which is over against Galilee. And when he went forth to land, there met him out of the city a certain man,

which had devils long time, and ware no clothes, neither abode in any house, but in the tombs. When he saw Jesus, he cried out, and fell down before him, and with a loud voice said, What have I to do with thee, Jesus, thou Son of God most high? I beseech thee, torment me not. (For he had commanded the unclean spirit to come out of the man. For oftentimes it had caught him: and he was kept bound with chains and in fetters; and he brake the bands, and was driven of the devil into the wilderness.) And Jesus asked him, saying, What is thy name? And he said Legion: because many devils were entered into him. And they besought him that he would not command them to go out into the deep. And there was there an herd of many swine feeding on the mountain: and they besought him that he would suffer them to enter into them. And he suffered them. Then went the devils out of the man, and entered into the swine: and the herd ran violently down a steep place into the lake, and were choked.

When they that fed them saw what was done, they fled, and went and told it in the city and in the country. Then they went out to see what was done; and came to Jesus, and found the man, out of whom the devils were departed, clothed, and in his right mind: and they were afraid. (St. Luke 8:26-35)

We had said above that the Devil, by way of demons, would enter the mind of a person and lead them to evil. As stated above, once the evilness is within a person, by way of the mind, the mind then begins to do evil things. Thus, one whose mind is without a diet of the truth that will set you free, would have a mind that wants to do wrong to others as well as the self. Then each person has to ask himself or herself, do I want to have a mind that does good to others, or do I want to destroy others? However, the biggest question is, do you realize that the Devil can make you do it? And if your answer is in the affirmative, then you have to find a way to deny the Devil in your mind. The above scripture says a diet consisting of Jesus will find the Devil kicked out of your mind and you in your right mind.

"THE" DIET FOR YOUR MIND TO HELP YOU FIND THE TRUTH THAT WILL SET YOU FREE

Why listen to Jesus? How can He tell me what to do and how to deal with the Devil? I'm glad you asked. The reason I listen to Jesus is because Jesus is the penicillin and the Devil is the infection. Thus, Jesus, the penicillin, can be used as protection from the Devil or, as stated above, as cure for the Devil. The above states how He acts as a cure, now let's see how he acts as protection from the Devil.

> Then was Jesus led up of the spirit into the wilderness to be tempted of the devil. And when he had fasted forty days and forty nights, he was afterward an hunger. And when the tempter came to him, he said, If thou be the Son of God, command that these stones be made bread. But he answered and said, It is written, Man shall not live by bread alone, but by every word that proceedeth out of the mouth of God. Then the devil taketh him up into the holy city, and setteth him on a pinnacle of the temple, And saith unto him, If thou be the Son of God, cast thyself down: for it is written, He shall give his angels charge concerning thee: and in their hands they shall bear thee up, lest at any time thou dash thy foot against a stone. Jesus said unto him, it is written again, Thou shalt not tempt the Lord thy God. Again the devil taketh him up into an exceeding high mountain, and sheweth him all the kingdoms of the world, and the glory of them; And saith unto him, All these things will I give thee, if thou wilt fall down and worship me. Then saith Jesus unto him, Get thee hence, Satan: for it is written, Thou shalt worship the Lord thy God, and him only shalt thou serve.
>
> Then the devil leaveth him, and, behold, angels came and ministered unto him. (St Matthew 4:1-11)

With the above truth, we find that Jesus used the Word of God to deny the devil access to his mind. The intelligent use of the Word of God is also available to His followers, those who have been born-again, as a weapon to defeat the devil. The intelligent use of the Word of God is to quote the scripture as it is written. Even though Adam and Eve didn't have the written word, they had the Word spoken to

THE TRINITY OF EVIL: LUCIFER, SATAN, AND THE DEVIL

them by God. So, when Eve responded with additional words other than what God said, she did not respond with the intelligent use of the Word.

> And the Lord God commanded the man, saying, Of every tree of the garden thou mayest freely eat: But of the tree of the knowledge of good and evil, thou shalt not eat of it: for in the day that thou eatest thereof thou shalt surely die. (Genesis 2:16-17)
>
> And the woman said unto the serpent, We may eat of the fruit of the trees of the garden; but of the fruit of the tree which is in the midst of the garden, God hath said, Ye shall not eat of it, neither shall ye touch it, lest ye die. (Genesis 3:2-3)

The above shows the contrast between what God said (the Word) and what Eve added to it with the statement, "Neither shall ye touch it, lest ye die." Eve didn't use the Word intelligently, because when she added the statement that she couldn't touch the tree, she was using God and her own words. So, part of using the Word intelligently is to say only what the Word says. This will defeat the Devil.

"THE" DIET FOR YOUR MIND TO HELP YOU FIND THE TRUTH THAT WILL SET YOU FREE

SUMMARY OF THE TRINITY OF EVIL

The above presentation of the Tri-evil was presented to help us understand more of what humanity is up against. Further, it is presented to give wisdom, knowledge and the truth that will allow humanity to know its enemy. Thus, regarding the Holy Trinity, we now know who the Father, Son and Holy Spirit are. They are one, and we know and understand the position and power of the evil-trinity.

As humanity, we know the Father was always in heaven until He came to earth in physical form as Jesus. Then, the Holy Spirit is like the wind, the air; He's everywhere.

The evil-trinity is the same. There is Lucifer, who is in the heavens. Remember he has access to the Father, evidenced at Job 1:6. When he appeared before God, with the sons of God, he did so as Satan, returning from earth as the accuser of humanity. Then as a spirit, or thought life, he is seen in humanity as demons or, collectively speaking, as the Devil.

With the above understanding of the trinity of evil, we need to have a holy understanding about one last thing. This goes beyond knowing when to rebuke Satan, the Devil or Lucifer, because we recognize which evil personality is at work, and goes to a truth that will make us free. That truth is that *humanity was given a body and dominion over the earth* (Genesis 1:26). The creator of earth gave the body and dominion over the earth to humanity. From a legal perspective, the earth, the body and dominion over the earth are owned fee simple. The Holy Trinity has absolute ownership.

What this means is the trinity of evil doesn't have a right to be present on earth. Lucifer as Satan and the Devil are trespassers. They trespassed in disguises, as in the Garden of Eden when he appeared as a serpent. Evil will appear as a person, when it has a human temple to appear in. We have seen this above when evil appeared with the name Legions, in the maniac of Gadara, the country of Gadarenes.

You may say, yes, evil appears by way of a human body, but why can't evil appear by way of a body? The response to this is that Good, the Holy Trinity, is the landlord (my Lord as well as my savior) of the body and the landlord has a right to visit, live in and control his property.

> For ye are bought with a price: therefore glorify God in your body, and in your spirit, which are God's. (I Corinthians 6:20)

> For God has bought you with a great price. So use every part of your body to give glory back to God, because he owns it. (I Corinthians 6:20 TLB)

Therefore, the Holy Trinity is working by and through humanity to reserve and protect His property. Whereas, the evil trinity is seeking to enter the property as a trespasser, and we know from common knowledge and experience that the trespasser always enters to do harm. The trespasser enters to steal, rob humanity of its birthright to be in the likeness of God. He enters to kill and to destroy the soul.

> The thief cometh not, but for to steal, and kill, and to destroy: I am come that they might have life, and that they might have it more abundantly. (St. John 10:10)

Thus, this final understanding of the battle of good against evil is that both work by, in, and through the person. However, evil is a trespasser and needs to be evicted from the person. If evil is to be evicted, then who are you going to call? That's simple, call the Landlord, the Holy Trinity. Then evil will have to defend possession of the body against the owner. If evil takes you to court on the charge of wrongful eviction, then he will lose. The reason being, he was a trespasser with no right to possess the body. Thus, his occupation of the body is unlawful, according to man and God's laws.

Finally, don't forget that your eviction of evil (Lucifer, Satan or the Devil) begins with putting your mind on a diet.

"THE" DIET FOR YOUR MIND TO HELP YOU FIND THE TRUTH THAT WILL SET YOU FREE

THE TRINITY OF CONSCIOUSNESSES

We have previously mentioned that man was originally created (spirit, body and soul) as an innocent being. However, he lost his original state after being disobedient and eating the forbidden fruit. By disobedience, man came to a personal and experimental knowledge of good and evil – of good as obedience, of evil as disobedience to the known will of God. Through the said knowledge, conscience awoke. We are reminded of the evidence that conscience was awakened because Adam and Eve hid themselves from God. This hiding was based upon shame, the shame of recognizing they were without clothes. However, before their disobedience, they had appeared before God naked and had no awareness of nakedness. Thus, when conscience was awoken, they became conscious of evil and there were three consciousnesses awoken. The three are God, world and self-consciousness. Let's visualize this:

GOD-CONSCIOUSNESS	WORLD-CONSCIOUSNESS	SELF-CONSCIOUSNESS
(SPIRIT)	(BODY)	(SOUL)
(MIND)	(THE FIVE SENSES)	(THE HEART)
The Spiritual Person	*The Natural Person*	*The Carnal Person*

Saint Paul in his effort to get others to understand the mind operating in persons, divided all human minds into three groups or consciousnesses. These consciousnesses would form the natures of people.[1]

The *spiritual* designates the renewed (born-again) person who walks in the Spirit: the person who is seeking God's way and is in full communion with God.

> And be not drunk with wine wherein excess; but be filled with the Spirit; Speaking to yourselves in psalms and hymns and making melody in your heart to the Lord; Giving thanks always for all things unto God and the Father in the name of our Lord Jesus Christ; (Ephesians 5:18-20)

THE TRINITY OF CONSCIOUSNESSES

The *natural* or *Adam-like* or *"senses"* person is a person who has not been renewed through the new birth (born-again) and lives for and of the world through his or her five senses.

> But the natural man receiveth not the things of the Spirit of God: for they are foolishness unto him: neither can he know them, because they are spiritually discerned. (I Corinthians 2:14)

The *carnal* or *fleshly* person is the person who has been born-again, has the new birth, but continues in walking *after the flesh, remains a babe in Christ and even though he is a Christian, is able to comprehend only its simplest truths, the milk of the Spirit.*

> And I, brethren, could not speak unto you as unto spiritual, but as unto carnal, even as unto babes in Christ. I have fed you with milk, and not with meat: for hitherto ye were not able to bear it, neither yet now are ye able. For ye are yet carnal: for whereas there is among you envying, and strife, and divisions, are ye not carnal, and walk as men? For while one saith, I am of Paul; and another, I am of Apollos; are ye not carnal? (I Corinthians 3:1-4)

We can conclude that Saint Paul has described the three types of persons. The first person is one who has only one birth. This person is called the natural person. Furthermore, this person's understanding comes through his or her five senses. He calls this person the natural person.

Then there are those who have been born-again; born of the Spirit. However, because this born-again person does not seek to walk in the spirit, or has not re-programmed or renewed the mind, this person's idiosyncrasies are similar to the natural person's, because the person looks to the flesh, the natural. St Paul calls this person a carnal or fleshly person.

The third type of person is called by St Paul the spiritual person. The spiritual person has been born-again and seeks to walk in the spirit; in the Word of God

"THE" DIET FOR YOUR MIND TO HELP YOU FIND THE TRUTH THAT WILL SET YOU FREE

1. GOD-CONSCIOUSNESS
(SPIRIT AND MIND)

In the dictionary, *conscience* is defined as the sense or consciousness of the moral goodness or blameworthiness of one's own conduct, intentions, or character, together with a feeling of obligation to do right or be good.

Conscious is defined as sharing knowledge or awareness of an inward state or outward fact, perceiving, apprehending, or noticing with a degree of controlled thought or observation.

When the third version of this word is defined, it is stated that *consciousness* is the quality or state of being aware especially of something within oneself, the totality of conscious states of an individual.

In summary of the above about conscience, being conscious and consciousness, it can be said that each person has a conscience. Previously it has been proven that this conscience came about because of the eating of the forbidden fruit, which involved disobeying the Creator. In the conscience, we find the free will of a person being tested. The test is to do good or to do evil. Thus, a person becomes conscious of his or her actions, the actions that the conscience says are good or evil.

The total reservoir of the conscience is the consciousness of an individual. This totality would be defined as the mind. The mind will determine the state of a person, what the person believes and guide him or her in this physical life.

We must recognize that because a person is partially spiritual, he or she is capable of God-consciousness and thereby able to communicate with God. This communication with God is by way of the mind. The mind, which is intangible, is fed through the mechanics of the brain. Later we will observe how the brain works. However, in an effort to understand the God-consciousness we have to realize that the mind will determine if a person will be obedient or disobedient to the known will of God.

Remember that above we stated that in 1 Corinthians 2:10-12 that persons have received the spirit of God. But, man was separated from God and His spirit because of disobedience. Thus, the free will of a person enables a will to disobey the Creator. The Spirit of God originating from man's creation is still within. However, what is being fed to the mind will determine if a person seeks the Spirit of God, the communication with God, and thereby develop his or her God-consciousness or rely upon his or her five senses.

2. WORLD-CONSCIOUSNESS (BODY AND FIVE SENSES)

Then there is the world-consciousness wherein the person's mind and spirit is fed from the five senses. The five senses – hearing, sight, touch, taste, and smell – are what the individual will rely on as the truth. However, there may have been several happenings which should have taught the person that the five senses are not reliable.

How many times, when advice is given about some con being played on citizens, do we hear the phrase, "If it sounds too good to be true, then it probably is too good to be true"? In other words, don't trust what you hear. Then, there was the time when the magician made the item disappear before the eyes. Later, another magician showed that the eyes were deceived.

The sense of taste should be the last sense to rely upon, especially given the number of artificial flavorings in products. However, the sense of feeling (touching) will be a close last when the reliability of the senses is recognized. The feelings are so vulnerable and so subject to manipulation and deceit.

When the sense of smell is called upon to provide a person with the truth, again the susceptibility comes up. There are certain cologne or perfumes that will not smell the same on one person as they do on another. The smell of a flower may differ as many times as there are persons to sample it. So, the sense of smell presents its own questionable odor.

"THE" DIET FOR YOUR MIND TO HELP YOU FIND THE TRUTH THAT WILL SET YOU FREE

THE SIXTH SENSE
(THE HOLY SPIRIT)

The five senses relate to the physical. However, later when we learn about the second birth we will discover the sixth sense. This sixth sense is no more than the use of God's knowledge and dependency on that knowledge as opposed to dependency on the five senses. It is the realization that the five senses can be deceived and thereby cause an individual to be deceived.

In the Holy Trinity, we say that the Holy Spirit will lead you into the wisdom, knowledge and truth that will set you free. So, when one has placed his five natural senses under the control and will of the Holy Spirit, he or she will have developed a sixth sense.

Jesus while speaking to multitudes would speak in parables. The natural mind, or a mind under the control and influence of the natural self and not the spirit, could not understand the spiritual message contained in the parables.

> But the man who isn't a Christian can't understand and can't accept these thoughts from God, which the Holy Spirit teaches us. They sound foolish to him, because only those who have the Holy Spirit *(the sixth sense)* within them can understand what the Holy Spirit means. Others just can't take it in. (I Corinthians 2:14 TLB)

3. SELF-CONSCIOUSNESS
(HEART: AFFECTIONS)

Whenever the heart is mentioned, as stated above, most will identify with the physical heart. However, in our quest to find the spiritual truth, we have learned that there is a physical body and a spiritual body. Also, there is a spiritual heart and a physical heart. The physical heart pumps blood, life, to the physical body. Then the spiritual heart pumps life to the spiritual body.

Furthermore, a person has to be aware of what is consumed to protect the heart from damage. We all have heard about cholesterol, blocked arteries and blocked heart valves. All of these and many more will damage the most essential part of the physical body.

Well, Jesus has told us above at St. Matthew 15 what type of cholesterol and what other things could cause spiritual blockage and eventual spiritual damage.

"THE" DIET FOR YOUR MIND TO HELP YOU FIND THE TRUTH THAT WILL SET YOU FREE

THE INTERACTION OF THE TRI-UNITY OF CONSCIOUSNESS

The above separate evaluations of the three consciousnesses were presented to make a person aware that it is though their conscience being conscious of the consciousnesses and through the consciousness of God, the world and the self, that a person is fed. That feeding will determine where he or she will spend eternity.

Furthermore, Lucifer is fighting God the Father to prevent a person from reaching God-consciousness. Satan is fighting Jesus for the control of the person's world-consciousness, and the Devil is fighting the Holy Spirit for the control of a person's self-consciousness.

> For we are not fighting against people made of flesh and blood, but against persons without bodies – the evil rulers of the unseen world, those mighty satanic beings and great evil princes of darkness who rule this world: and against huge numbers of wicked spirits in the spirit world. (Ephesians 6:12 TLB)

Humanity was created in the spiritual world, with a spiritual soul and a physical body. When he committed the act of disobedience, he left his original state and was kicked out of his home. Now, he needs to get back home. However, there are forces fighting within him; one is trying to get man back home and the other is trying to convince man to accept another place. This battle is between the forces of good and evil. These forces originate in the spirit world. Jehovah is God of good and Lucifer the god of evil.

We have seen in the Manual where it is mentioned about one who sought to overthrow the ruler, God, in heaven, to take God's place and thereby to rule heaven and the heavenly host. He believed that by taking over heaven he would also rule over God's colony, earth.

He failed in his coup d'état and then sought to rule over earth. Thus, he appeared as a serpent in the beautiful Garden of Eden. Note that he probably fitted in with the beauty of the garden; because the word is that the serpent was one of the most beautiful creatures.

Anyway, Lucifer, being a spiritual being, was seeking the human being who had been given dominion over the earth. He wanted to teach the human being to be like him – to be kicked out of his home. Lucifer, with the knowledge of how to be disobedient, taught humans from experience. Misery loves company. If I can't have, you shouldn't have: I, I, and I; the self, self, self wanting others to be like the self. The self, Lucifer, was initially successful and the human beings, Adam and Eve, were kicked out of their home, the Garden of Eden.

One further truth must be recognized when recognizing that the human beings were kicked out of their home. We must recognize that when Lucifer was kicked out of the heavenly court, he lost a certain relationship with the Father. Well, when Adam and Eve were kicked out of the Garden of Eden, they lost a certain relationship with the Father. It is through the body that the soul and spirit have world-consciousnesses. The spirit and soul work through the body while the body exists. Again, it is very important to remember that the contaminated soul exists, which needs to be decontaminated in each living creature. Thus, a person's emotions, desires, affection, active will, a person's self, must be decontaminated. The decontamination has to begin with a diet, a diet for the mind, the mind that will control all consciousnesses.

I am reminded here of an e-mail I received from one of my co-workers. I don't know the author, but the content of the e-mail is appropriate here.

> An old Cherokee is teaching his grandson about life. "A fight is going on inside me," he said to the boy. "It is a terrible fight and it is between two wolves.
>
> One is evil – he is anger, envy, sorrow, regret, greed, arrogance, self-pity, guilt, resentment, inferiority, lies, false pride, superiority, and ego.
>
> The other is good – he is joy, peace, love, hope, serenity, humility, kindness, benevolence, empathy, generosity, truth, compassion, and faith.
>
> This same fight is going on inside you – and inside every other person too."

"THE" DIET FOR YOUR MIND TO HELP YOU FIND THE TRUTH THAT WILL SET YOU FREE

The grandson thought about it for a minute and then asked his grandfather, "Which wolf will win?"

The old Cherokee replied, "The one you feed."

YOUR PERSONAL COMPUTER OF MAN (P.C.M.)
AND
YOUR PERSONAL COMPUTER OF GOD (P.C.S.)

One of the greatest inventions the human has invented, developed and placed into use is the computer, the computer in general and the personal computer (PC). This is what I call the personal computer of man (PCM). Then there is the personal computer of spirit (PCS) that was created by God the Spirit.

The computer, PCM or otherwise, as we all know, has an existence founded upon being an instrument to handle information or data. Computers gather, store and await usage of data.

There is different usage of the stored information. Since there is different information and different use of the information, there had to be developed a means of storage and usage. Thus, there had to be developed what are called programs. There is a program used for accounting. A different program is used for word processing. Then inasmuch as there are drafts to be used, a program for drafting was developed.

The PCM owes its existence and working to the PCS, because the computer was founded upon the principals of the working of the human brain and mind, which are the human's PCS. Thus, as one's PCM will operate according to the program activated, so will one's PCS. The results will depend on the program. The program used will depend on the programmer. The program used in your PCM may be designed by Microsoft, Intel or other human programmers. However, your PCS is designed with the spiritual program of God but can be contaminated with the spirit of evil. So, we can say that we have reached the conclusion that there are similarities between the PCM and the PCS.

Believe it or not, your PCM is founded upon the same operational principles as your PCS; after all, there is nothing new under the sun. The PCM, to perform its functions, has a mainframe, hard drive, keyboard, mouse, monitor, A, B, or C drives, a CD-Rom and a printer. There are components of the PCS that perform various functions. Furthermore, when the functions of each of these

"THE" DIET FOR YOUR MIND TO HELP YOU FIND THE TRUTH THAT WILL SET YOU FREE

components are explored, we can find similar components in the PCS and PCM performing similar functions.

The following is a visual demonstration of how the PCM and PCS are similar in their functions.

THE PCM	THE PCS
THE MAINFRAME	THE HUMAN BRAIN
(THE HARD & OTHER DRIVES)	(THE MIND)
THE KEY BOARD	THE HUMAN FIVE SENSES
THE MOUSE	THE INDIVIDUAL FIVE SENSES
THE MONITOR	THE HUMAN EYES
THE C.D.ROM	THE HUMAN EMOTIONS
THE PRINTER	THE HUMAN RESPONSES

The above provides a visual explanation that indeed the PCS is the prototype used to create and operate the PCM.

The mainframe of the PCM is where ability to perform any function is located. It's where the physical chips and all other needed hardware is located. On the other hand, the body's mainframe is the human brain. The brain is where the human physical hardware, the cerebrum, cerebellum, and all the other tangible tools needed to allow the operation of the brain, exist. Thus, the brain makes it possible for the intangible mind to exist.

The hard drive and other drives in the P.C. are databases, sources that performs the function of giving and receiving information. The human brain receives and stores data by way of all of the five senses. Then, when inquiries are received, the response will depend on the data stored.

The keyboard of the PCS is the five senses. It is the senses that see, smell, taste, hear and feel. The five senses feed the hard drive and other drives. Then, when the senses come into contact with a similar experience, the brain responds using the data stored. In other words, the keyboard is used to give and receive data.

The mouse of the PCM is an individual sense giving and receiving data. The mouse allows for a quicker response. Also, the mouse is usually used without the keyboard. Thus, the keyboard allows the

YOUR PERSONAL COMPUTER OF MAN (P.C.M.) AND
YOUR PERSONAL COMPUTER OF GOD (P.C.S.)

simultaneous working of all senses, whereas, the mouse may be one of five senses or several working together.

The eyes are one of the five senses that the mind relies upon for data. So, in the PCS, the eyes are the monitors. They see what's being placed in, taken out, or observed and viewed.

We could say that the mind is the spiritual (intangible) part to the brain. It is the intangible, which is fed by way of what an individual sees, hears, smells, tastes or feels.

When the human brain is functioning it has many areas to receive and store info (data). The A B and C drives are the PC's storage source. However, when the brain is gathering, storing or releasing data, the same is accomplished in the mind.

The CD-Rom is an independent storage source, which has its own information. It can usually operate independently of the hard drive. So, we can say that the CD-Rom of the PCS is the five senses in the PCS operating without the individual's five senses doing any evaluation. This is commonly called a voluntary response. This voluntary response, as we will observe later, will depend on programming. There will be an observation of the environment that presents the stimulus, and the emotions, responses, will appear. An example could be the observation of hate and the option to respond with hate or love. The observation can be followed with a response of prejudice, or the response of a brother or sister to the person. Again, the brain receives the observation, but the mind will determine the response.

The PCM prints to provide a means to visualize data. The human's eye in the PCS is used to visualize data.

The following will concentrate on the components that receive store and give information. Thus, the concentration will be on the mainframe (the human brain), the hard and other drives (the human mind), the keyboard (the total five senses) and the monitor (the human eyes).

"THE" DIET FOR YOUR MIND TO HELP YOU FIND THE TRUTH THAT WILL SET YOU FREE

THE MIND AND THE COMPUTER

We have said that one of the greatest inventions humans have invented, developed, and placed in use is the computer. Also, the computer's existence is founded upon working with information. Information is gathered and stored and awaits usage. There are different types of information and different uses of information. Since there are differences in types of information and their storage and usage, we have to develop what is called programming.

Programming, simply put, is the means by which computers receive, analyze and display information. So a program for accounting will differ from a program for word-processing.

In accounting the primary task is to work with numbers. A spreadsheet will be needed in the accounting program. The word-processor's program is created primarily to work with words. So, a spreadsheet is replaced in the word-processing programming with an ability to handle words.

Well, we have come to realize that the human brain, the PCS, is the creator of the PCM. Furthermore, like the PCM, the PCS is capable of using programs. Thus, the program in use will determine the printout, the human response.

When we come to the human brain, we are concerned with programming. The spreadsheet program, as well as the word-processing program, takes place in the PCS. Thus, when all the programming is spoken of as a whole, we have the mind.

We have concluded in past chapters that the mind is the results of programming found in the brain. The brain, having received the potential of two opposing programs, good and evil, creates a mind with a potential for good and evil. The body has the same potential – the potential to be at a proper weight or overweight. Furthermore, we have concluded that the way for the physical body to avoid being overweight would be to go on a diet – not only a diet of watching what you eat and how much you eat, but a diet that includes exercises.

In an effort to lose weight or avoid being overweight, we buy certain machines, special foods and unique clothing, and we spend a lot of time exercising. All this and more is done for a physical body which aches with pain and one day will return to dust, from whence it came.

In the first chapter, we were trying to determine how to put the mind on a diet. The above means of physical dieting would be used for a physical diet. However, where do I find a diet and exercises to place my mind on a diet? We have concluded that God made the brain, which allows a mind, the conscience of good and evil. The PCS is the basis of the PCM. Thus, we can understand that the results of a PCM will depend on its programming, and that the same must be true of the PCS. In recognition of this truth, consistency, the Manual for the PCS is the only place to find the PCS's programming.

Anyone will tell you that the first step in dieting is to have a desire for change. As previously mentioned, in physical dieting there must be a change in the physical and mental state if the dieting is to be successful in accomplishing the desired results. The desired results sought from a physical diet are to lose weight or to prevent too much weight being gained. The desired results sought with a mind diet are to lose and prevent evil thoughts while at the same time replacing these thoughts with good thoughts. The good thoughts are the thoughts that are results of God, the Father, the Son and the Holy Spirit's way; the evil thoughts are the thoughts of Lucifer, Satan or the Devil's way.

We can go on to say that the reason there must be a mind diet is because of contamination. The contamination is of Lucifer. This contaminant came with each person born of Adam and Eve. Thus, the contamination is a factory one, born into each living soul and passed on to each son and daughter from generation to generation. The contamination is called sin, disobedience to the word of God. It's in our nature; it is that which comes naturally.

"THE" DIET FOR YOUR MIND TO HELP YOU FIND THE TRUTH THAT WILL SET YOU FREE

THE SECOND BIRTH
(BORN-AGAIN)

As I continued consulting the Manual to take steps to place my mind on a diet, the following was found:

> Jesus answered and said unto him, Verily, verily, I say unto thee, Except a man be born again, he cannot see the kingdom of God.
>
> Jesus answered, verily, verily, I say unto thee, Except a man be born of water and of the Spirit, he cannot enter into the kingdom of God. That which is born of the flesh is flesh; and that which is born of the Spirit is spirit. (St. John 3:3,5-6)
>
> Only the Holy Spirit gives eternal life. Those born only once, with physical birth, will never receive the gift. But now I have told you how to get this true spiritual life. (St John 6:63)

There could be a whole book written on the kingdom of God. The Reverend Scofield in his footnotes to St. Matthew 6:33[1] states the kingdom of God is universal. It includes all mortal intelligences willingly subject to the will of God, whether angels, the Church, or saints of past or future dispensations; while the kingdom of heaven is Messianic, mediatorial, and Davidic, and has for its object the establishment of the kingdom of God in the earth. The Kingdom of God is entered only by the new birth.

Now every kingdom must have a king.

> Then Pilate entered into the judgment hall again, and called Jesus, and said unto him, Art thou the King of the Jews?
>
> Jesus answered, My kingdom is not of this world; if my kingdom were of this world, then would my servants fight, that I should not be delivered to the Jews: but now is my kingdom not from hence. (St John 18:33,36)

Jesus came to get living souls back to the kingdom of God by way of establishing the kingdom of heaven on earth. So the kingdom

THE SECOND BIRTH (BORN-AGAIN)

would be on earth, but not of the earth. (That which is flesh is flesh, born of the flesh, and that which is spirit must be born of the spirit). Furthermore, the transformation that is needed, according to the Manual, is found in the meaning of transformation itself, change.

When I think of change I can remember my two children in their growing years. My daughter, Shronda, when she became thirteen or fourteen years of age, called me one day. In our discussion, which I believe to have been about a curfew, she made a statement that called for a change: "Dad, I am fourteen years old and you are treating me as if I am still a kid." Of course, my first response was she was a kid and would always be my kid.

Then I realized what she was saying was true. My approach to her was dad to child. I had failed to realize that a child would grow. I had given her milk as an infant, but now she was in need of solid food. If I wanted to take care of my teenager, would milk be the only food I provided? Or, would so-called solid food be fed to her. The answer was solid food. Then it stood to reason that as her physical diet had changed, so her spirit and mind had changed. Therefore, I could no longer look upon her or communicate with her as dad to infant; I had to communicate with her as dad to a young lady.

I could have never reached the conclusion to change my approach to relating to her without first realizing that a change was needed. My next response was to say she was right in her analysis of my approach to her. I requested several days to reprogram my mind.

In about seven or eight days I called my daughter and we began a new relationship. This was a relationship based upon person to person, dad to child and friend-to-friend.

My son, LaGuardia, has also helped me to grow in the area of change. When he was about seven, as the typical little boy, he wanted a dog. I explained that I would get him a dog if the dog remained outside. Furthermore, I explained to him that I wasn't a dog lover. However, because my love for him was greater than my lack of love for dogs, he could have a dog.

A co-worker had heard that I was looking for a puppy for my son. She mentioned that a dog, which belonged to her friend, had just had puppies. Furthermore, the friend would probably give my son one of the puppies. My son and I visited the co-worker's friend one afternoon. She allowed my son the opportunity to pick from the litter. He chose the only puppy that was totally black. We were told that the mother of the puppies was a Dalmatian and the father unknown. However, most had said from observing the size of the paws, and the color of the hair, that the father appeared to have been a Labrador. My son named the puppy Pongo, from the 101 Dalmatian Movie.

Well, since I wasn't a dog lover and I was only allowing Pongo out of my love for my son, I made some strict rules. First, Pongo couldn't come into the house. That rule was overruled the first day. Next, the dog couldn't come upstairs in the house. This rule was broken the first night. Pongo couldn't sleep in his bed. The first night when he was taken upstairs, where do you think he slept? Soon my last rule, the dog was not to come into my room, was broken.

About six months later, Pongo wasn't with us any longer. We purchased a cocker spaniel and he died two weeks later. Then we purchased Angel, another cocker spaniel. Needless to say, no rules were given, other than for feeding, walking and other care-taking rules. However, I must confess that now I know what a person means when they say they have no children, but a dog or cat. Or, when the statement is made that the pet is like one of the family. Also, I have observed the three puppies my son had. In observing, I have come to realize that there is something in them that we call instinct, like the instinct to scratch the earth, or in Angel's case, the carpet. Even though she has been a house pet since she was four weeks old, she would approach an area to lie down. But, before she lay down, she would scratch the area she was going to lie in.

My observation of Angel has helped me to understand that there is something inside Angel that makes her prep for lying down. This preparation, scratching into the surface, was done on floors of tile or carpet, where there would be no change in the surface. However, Angel had in her nature the mind to do what came to her, the thing that was in her seed. The thing would make her scratch, whether there was a movable surface or not. The nature of Angel was to scratch the surface before lying down.

My daughter and son have taught me that there is a time when change is needed. This can be a change in how we observe others. It can be a change that leads one to accept something that one used to be

THE SECOND BIRTH (BORN-AGAIN)

totally against. Also, Angel and her two predecessors taught me that unless there was a change in the mind, there was no change. In other word, you could take the dog out of nature (outside) but you couldn't take the nature out of the dog. However, you must take the dog out when another part of nature calls.

When Jesus said you must be born-again, he was saying there must be a change. A person born of flesh has experienced their natural birth, the birth to their earthly parents. However, as long as one has only the earthly birth, the physical birth, one can only see earthly things, and therefore only natural things (earthy things) are understood. (That which is flesh understands only the flesh.) Thus, the natural person will understand the natural, and because the natural seed has become contaminated, there can be no understanding of the truth that will set you free.

The episode of being born-again, the second birth, will be a birth whereby a person is born of the spirit ("And that which is born of Spirit is spirit"). The spirit will understand the spirit. This understanding will lead to the restoration of man to God. It will result in a person seeking God-consciousnesses and not the world-consciousnesses or self-consciousnesses. A person born of the Spirit will walk in the Spirit. This is achieved only by the person renewing his or her mind.

> I BESEECH you therefore, brethren, by the mercies of God, that ye present your bodies a living sacrifice, holy, acceptable unto God, which is your reasonable service.
>
> And be not conformed to this world: but be ye transformed by the renewing of your mind, that ye may prove what is that good, and acceptable and perfect, will of God. (Romans 12:1-2)

The Manual says there must be a transforming, a renewing of my mind. The renewing would be accomplished by a mental diet, which will cause a change in my thought life; the thought life has to be of the Spirit of God to be able to discern the will of God.

The diet of feeding on the Spirit, the Word of God, enabled me first to realize that I am a spirit. Even though I have a physical body, I am also a spirit. As a spiritual being, I can't rely on just the physical.

"THE" DIET FOR YOUR MIND TO HELP YOU FIND THE TRUTH THAT WILL SET YOU FREE

The physical is natural. My natural self (natural mind) has been damaged. Thus, its information can't be relied upon for the total person. I must seek the spirit, that which is of God.

I can remember as a young boy being compelled to go to church on Sundays by my parents. On almost each visit, there would be an old sister who would give the testimony about how she found God. Furthermore, since she had found God, she had changed. Now she had a new walk, a new talk and new feet, which came with the new hands. We young ones would look at each other and say the hands, feet, talk and walk were the same to us. Thus, after participating in the laughter, we didn't hear the conclusions of her testimony.

Finally, I asked my mother why would these old ladies say they had new this and that when we all still saw the same old hands, feet and walk and heard the same old mouth say some of the same old things?

Mom in her patient way explained the expressions by these older women as being the expressions of a person born-again. On the outside we saw the same old feet, hands, and walk. However, Sister Jones was saying there had been a change in the inside, where the true change is needed. She was saying that since she had been born-again, she still had the old feet as seen by the physical eye, but if she were viewed with a spiritual eye the spirit would show her feet walking in the spirit, doing things according to the spirit, as opposed to doing things of the world or only in consideration of herself.

Yes, she had the same old physical hands, but the spiritual hands would now reach out to others in an effort to help others, and would not seek to destroy others. Her mouth sought to say only the good about others and if no good could be said, nothing was said at all.

When I entered the ministry, there was a big thing about being born-again. I sought to understand the expression "You must be born-again." Yes, I read the above scripture in the Manual, but reading is one thing, understanding is another. I asked others to explain what "born-again" meant. A number of fellow Christians shared with me their understanding. However, I sought a spiritual understanding.

I was like Nicodemus when Jesus told him that except a man is born-again, he couldn't see the kingdom of God.

THE SECOND BIRTH (BORN-AGAIN)

Jesus answered and said unto him, Verily, verily, I say unto thee, Except a man be born again, he cannot see the Kingdom of God.

Nicodemus saith unto him, How can a man be born when he is old? Can he enter the second time into his mother's womb, and be born? (St. John 3:3-4)

There is in the Manual a scripture that states, "Seek and ye shall find." I have experienced this to be true. I was seeking with my spirit to understand what Jesus was saying to Nicodemus. Then one day I had turned on the radio to hear a favorite preacher of mine. He probably didn't know me, but God had used him and many others to place this mind on a diet and become a renewed mind. Although he was more of a teacher, the preacher explained being "born-again" this way. He simply spoke as Jesus often would to teach a lesson. He taught me the lesson on the new birth by telling me about the caterpillar and butterfly.

There is a creature that is first born as a worm. This worm is called a caterpillar. As a caterpillar, the creature crawls on its belly. Then there is something that happens. This crawling caterpillar crawls up on a limb of a plant and goes through metamorphosis. At the completion of its metamorphosis (change), he leaves the limb of the plant. No, he doesn't crawl further up the limb, nor does he crawl down. Well, how does he leave the limb? He flies away. You see, that which was a crawling worm has changed (gone through metamorphosis) and is now a new creature. It has "transformed" from one thing to being a totally different thing; nevertheless, because of its origin it is the same creature.

Later I would view the caterpillar as a crawling creature, which farmers hate, because often the caterpillar would destroy the crops and plants. However, the farmer and gardeners would love the butterfly because it would bring life to plants, mostly beautiful flowers. Another metaphoric aspect of this creature was its appearances. The caterpillar is considered to be ugly and crawls slowly. On the other hand, the butterfly comes in such picturesque colors and flies with beauty and grace.

The above has explained the metamorphosis of the caterpillar. However, the second birth (change) of the human needs to be understood. In the theologian's hall, the new birth is called regeneration.

Dr. Scofield describes the regeneration in his footnotes to St. John 3:3.[2] He says the necessity of the new birth grows out of the incapacity of the natural man to "see" or "enter into" the kingdom of God. "However gifted, moral, or refined, the natural man is absolutely blind to spiritual truth, and impotent to enter the kingdom; for he can neither obey, understand, nor please God....The new birth is not a reformation of the old nature...but a creative act of the Holy Spirit."

> For they that are after the flesh do mind the things of the flesh; but they that are after the Spirit the things of the Spirit.
> Because the carnal mind is enmity against God: for it is not subject to the law of God, neither indeed can be. So they that are in the flesh cannot please God. (Romans 8:5,7-8)

Scofield goes on to say that, "The condition of the new birth is faith in Christ crucified... Through the new birth, the believer becomes a partaker of the divine nature and of the life of Christ Himself."[3]

> But ye are not in the flesh, but in the Spirit, if so be that the Spirit of God dwell in you. Now if any man have not the Spirit of Christ, he is none of his. And if Christ be in you, the body is dead because of sin; but the Spirit is life because of righteousness. But if the Spirit of him that raised up Jesus from the dead dwell in you, he that raised up Christ from the dead shall also quicken your mortal bodies by his Spirit that dwelleth in you. (Romans 8: 9-11)

The apostle Paul, as mentioned above, identifies humans in three categories. There is the "carnal" which Paul would call "fleshly" and the carnal or fleshly person is a person who seeks the pleasures of the flesh even though the person has been born again.

The second type or category of humanity Paul calls the "natural" – those un-renewed through the new birth. In other words, this type of person doesn't live just for and by way of the five senses. This person would be considered as a person who might do good deeds.

THE SECOND BIRTH (BORN-AGAIN)

Nevertheless, this person doesn't recognize the need for a second birth. Thus, since there is no second birth (spiritual birth), the spiritual content of the Manual or the Word of God is absolutely hidden from the natural person.

Then there is the "spiritual" person, the person identified as a renewed person who is Spirit filled; this person has been born-again and now seeks after the Spirit, and walks in the Spirit in full communion with God. This one has gone beyond world-consciousness (the five senses) and beyond self-consciousness (lacking the understanding to do to others what they would want to be done unto them) and found God-consciousness, the desire to be whole. There is a recognition that the PCS was contaminated, had a virus, and had to be renewed and reprogrammed to find the way back to his original state, the Spirit.

"THE" DIET FOR YOUR MIND TO HELP YOU FIND THE TRUTH THAT WILL SET YOU FREE

HOW TO BE BORN A SECOND TIME (BORN-AGAIN)

Now that I knew I needed a second birth, I went back to Nicodemus. How would I achieve this?

> And no man hath ascended up to heaven, but he that came down from heaven, even the Son of man, which is in heaven. And as Moses lifted up the serpent in the wilderness, even so must the Son of man be lifted up: That whosoever believeth in him should not perish, but have eternal life. St. (John 3:13-15)

This regenerated person is said to be saved. You may ask, "From what is the person saved?" Remember in the above chapter, we spoke of what would be saved. It is the soul of the person that will be saved. (If you have forgotten the chapter, please refresh your mind.) We said therein that the soul of a person is what will live on. It was the soul that became contaminated and needed renewing. Thus, when one has accepted Christ, one becomes born of the Spirit, and the Spirit of God begins to be the dominant force in one's life. One's emotions are beyond the physical and sin driven. They are walking in the Spirit.

The person who is "saved" has salvation. When a person is saved, he or she will experience salvation. Therefore, salvation means the person is saved from guilt and the penalty of sin, the habit and dominion of sin, and is saved in the sense that the person is now capable of conforming entirely to Christ.

Salvation is by grace through faith, salvation is a free gift, and wholly without works.

> For by grace are ye saved through faith; and that not of yourselves: it is the gift of God: not of works, lest any man should boast. (Ephesians 2:8-9)

We have often heard of the word *Grace*. *Grace* could be defined as the kindness and love of God our Savior toward man. The Webster Dictionary would define *grace* as unmerited divine assistance given man for his regeneration or sanctification, a virtue coming from God.

In the Manual, *grace* is considered to be one on the dispensations. Remember in the earlier chapter, we spoke of innocence and conscience as dispensations. We further stated that a dispensation is a period of time during which man's obedience to some specific revelation of the will of God is tested. The dispensation of grace followed the dispensation of law.

The dispensation of law began with God speaking to Moses to tell the people of Israel of his desire.

> In the third month, when the children of Israel were gone forth out of the land of Egypt, the same day came they into the wilderness of Sinai. For they were departed from Rephidim, and were come to the desert of Sinai, and had pitched in the wilderness; and there Israel camped before the mount. And Moses went up unto God, and the Lord called unto him out of the mountain, saying, Thus shalt thou say to the house of Jacob, and tell the children of Israel; Ye have seen what I did unto the Egyptians, and how I bare you on eagles' wings, and brought you unto myself. Now therefore, if ye will obey my voice indeed, and keep my covenant, then ye shall be a peculiar treasure unto me above all people: for all the earth is mine: And ye shall be unto me a kingdom of priests, and an holy nation. These are the words which thou shalt speak unto the children of Israel. And Moses came and called for the elders of the people, and laid before their faces all these words which the Lord commanded him. And all the people answered together, and said, All that the Lord hath spoken we will do. And Moses returned the words of the people unto the Lord. (Exodus 19:1-8)

Along with the dispensation of law, which is found at the twentieth chapter of Exodus comes the Mosaic Covenant. A covenant is an agreement between individuals or peoples, and more particularly between individuals or peoples, and God, involving the formality of a binding oath and some ritual of witness.

> And when Abram was ninety years old and nine, the Lord appeared to Abram, and said unto him, I am the Almighty God; walk before me, and be thou perfect. And I will make my covenant between me and

thee, and will multiply thee exceedingly. And Abram fell on his face; and God talked with him, saying, As for me, behold, my covenant is with thee, and thy shall be a father of many nations. Neither shall thy name any more be called Abram; but thy name shall be Abraham; for a father of many nations have I made thee. And I will make thee exceedingly fruitful, and I will make nations of thee, and kings shall come out of thee. And I will establish my covenant between me and thee and thy seed after thee in their generations for an everlasting covenant, to be a God unto thee, and to thy seed after thee. And I will give unto thee, and to thy seed after thee, the land wherein thou art a stranger, all the land of Canaan, for an everlasting possession; and I will be their God. And God said unto Abraham, Thou shall keep my covenant therefore, thou and thy seed after thee in their generations. This is my covenant, which ye shall keep, between me and you and thy seed after thee; Every man child among you shall be circumcised. And ye shall circumcise the flesh of your foreskin; and it shall be a token of the covenant betwixt me and you. (Genesis 17:1-11)

The dispensation is a short time of testing an individual or mankind. The covenant is everlasting. The covenant God made with Abraham did not end when Moses Covenant was given. Only the dispensation of testing Israel ended. The covenant between Abraham and God was extended to include the non-Israelite nations, as God has covenanted with Abraham.

The dispensation of grace, which began with the death and resurrection of Christ, is a contrast to the dispensation of law. When these two dispensations are compared, the difference leaps out even to the un-renewed mind. An examination will show that which "under law" was a "condition," is "under grace" "freely given" to every believer (everyone who has the second birth.) Under the law, God demands righteousness from man, as under grace he gives righteousness to man. The law is connected with Moses and work; grace with Christ and faith. The law blesses those that are good; grace saves those who are bad. If under the law there is to be any blessings, law demands that the blessings be earned; grace is a free gift from God. The law requires a sacrifice for sin, the shedding of blood. We will find under the law the shedding of animal blood for each sin. Then there had to be a certain animal for a particular sin. However, under grace Jesus shed his blood for all sins.

Again, grace, as a dispensation, begins with the death and resurrection of Christ. Thus, grace ended the testing of legal obedience as the condition of salvation, and changed the condition to the acceptance of Christ. It made good works the fruit of salvation. Under the law, good works would earn salvation.

> In the beginning was the Word, and the Word was with God, and the Word was God. The same was in the beginning with God. All things were made by him; and without him was not any thing made that was made. In him was life; and the life was the light of men.
>
> That was the true Light, which lighteth every man that cometh into the world. He was in the world, and the world was made by him, and the world knew him not. He came unto his own, and his own received him not. But as many as received him, to them gave he power to become the sons of God, even to them that believe on his name; Which were born, not of blood, nor of the will of the flesh, nor of the will of man, but of God. And the Word was made flesh, and dwelt among us, (and we beheld his glory, the glory as of the only begotten of the Father,) full of grace and truth. (St. John 1:1-4, 9-14)
>
> But the righteousness which is of faith speaketh on this wise, Say not in thine heart, Who shall ascend into heaven? (that is, to bring Christ down from above:) Or, Who shall descend into the deep? (that is, to bring up Christ again from the dead.) But what saith it? The word is nigh thee, even in thy mouth, and in thy heart: that is, the word of faith, which we preach: That if thou shalt confess with thy mouth the Lord Jesus, and shalt believe in thine heart that God hath raised him from

the dead, thou shalt be saved. For with the heart man believeth unto righteousness; and with the mouth confession is made unto salvation. For whosoever shall call upon the name of the Lord shall be saved. (Romans 10:6-10,13)

The above scriptures from the Manual have outlined our diet for the mind. There is an affirmation that Jesus, while walking on this earth, was God in the flesh. Under the law, there were only prophets, which were given the word for obedience to the law from God. However, when Jesus came, he was God himself telling of God. Again, we are back to the Holy Trinity, as mentioned in an above chapter. Anyway, there remains the question, how does the second birth happen?

THE NEW COVENANT

The above portion of the Manual at Chapter 17 in Genesis shows the covenant God made with the nation of Israel, of which Abraham became the father. This is said to be the "Old Covenant." Yes, there were other covenants made between God and man. There is the Edenic Covenant, or the covenant made between Adam, Eve and God in the Garden of Eden. This was the first of the eight great covenants in the Manual, which condition life and salvation. The Adamic Covenant, made with Adam, conditioned the life of fallen man. The Noahic Covenant, between God and Noah, made after the great flood, confirmed the relationship of man to the earth, as stated in the Adamic Covenant. The next two covenants are the Abrahamic, which God made with Abraham, and Mosaic, which was made with Moses, as stated above. The sixth, the Palestinian Covenant, sets out the conditions under which Israel would enter the land of promise. The seventh covenant, the Davidic Covenant, is the covenant made between God and David that the kingdom of Christ would be found through David's family.

The eighth covenant is known as the New Covenant.

The old agreement didn't even work. If it had, there would have been no need for another to replace it. But God himself found fault with the old one, for he said, "The day will come when I will make a new agreement with the people of Israel and the people of Judah. This new agreement will not be like the old one I gave to their fathers on the day when I took them by the hand to lead them out of the land of Egypt; they did not keep their part in that agreement, so I had to cancel it. But this is the new agreement I will make with the people of Israel, says the Lord: I will write my laws in their minds so that they will know what I want them to do without even telling them, and these laws will be in their hearts so that they will want to obey them, and I will be their God and they shall be my people. And no one then will need to speak to his friend or neighbor or

brother, saying, 'You, too, should know the Lord,' because everyone, great and small, will know me already. And I will be merciful to them in their wrongdoings, and I will remember their sins no more."
God speaks of these new promises, of the new agreement, as taking the place of the old one; for the old one is out of date now and has been put aside forever. (Hebrews 8:7-13 TLB)

Now you can see why the preceding chapters are significant. The above scripture focuses upon a new agreement, a covenant, wherein God would not rely upon his printed word on stone. Rather he would print his word in the heart and mind of man. God would not seek to communicate with man from the outside to the inside. Since, it's the inside that is of importance, God decided to make an agreement to live inside and fight for change where change was needed.

The New Covenant is the covenant in which you and I could enter into today. But you may say, "The above covenants were made between God and Adam, God and Noah, and God and the Nation of Israel, through men of Hebrew (Israeli) decent. Therefore, how can a non-Israelite claim any portion of the promise that was made to the Nation of Israel? Where in the Manual does it state that a non-Israelite is a part and partaker of the new agreement?"

To understand how the non-Israelite can receive the blessings promised to Abraham and his seed, we must review the Manual from the time of creation. When the first man, Adam, was created and until God made the Covenant with Abram, who became Abraham, there was no Jew or Gentile; all had been one in the first man, Adam. When God made the covenant with Abraham, he made a promise of a nation. This nation would be called Israel. Thus, all of the covenants made with mankind from the Abraham Covenant to the beginning of the New Covenant were made with the nation of Israel. Therefore, the earthly race, which was not a part of the Israelites, was known as Gentiles. Then, when the New Covenant went into effect, the death and resurrection of Jesus Christ, the earthly race was divided into Jews (Israelites), Gentiles and Christians. This is how God sees all earthly living beings, as Gentiles, Jews or Christians.

THE NEW COVENANT

Please be aware that the division of humanity into Gentiles, Jews and Christians here is mentioned to show how God sees humanity from Adam to Christ in terms of covenants. Furthermore, there was one covenant God made with Adam and all others were made with the Jews, until the New Covenant. God makes the New Covenant with all humanity. Through Christ and in Christ, the New Covenant says, "Come Gentiles, come Jews, and become as one, as Christians."

Today the Gentiles would include any living being who is not a Jew or a Christian. The Jew would be a living being who is a descendant of Abraham, who is the father of the Jewish nation. A Christian would be anyone who has accepted Christ as his or her Lord and Savior, Gentile or Jew.

> Long ago, even before he made the world, God chose us to be his very own, through what Christ would do for us: he decided then to make us holy in his eyes, without a single fault – we who stand before him covered with love. His unchanging plan has always been to adopt us into his own family by sending Jesus Christ to die for us. And he did this because he wanted to! (Ephesians 1:4-5 TLB)
>
> That the blessing of Abraham might come on to the Gentiles through Jesus Christ; that we might receive the promise of the Spirit through faith. (Galatians 3:14)
>
> Now God can bless the Gentiles, too, with this same blessing he promised to Abraham; and all of us as Christians can have the promised Holy Spirit through this faith. Dear brothers, even in everyday life a promise made by one man to another, if it is written down and signed, cannot be changed. He cannot decide afterward to do something else instead.
>
> Now God gave some promises to Abraham and his Child. And notice that it doesn't say the promise were made to his children, as it would if all his sons – all Jews – were being spoken of, but to his Child – and that of course, means Christ.
>
> Here's what I am trying to say: God's promise to save through faith – and God wrote this promise down

and signed it – could not be canceled or changed four hundred and thirty years later when God gave the Ten Commandments. If obeying those laws could save us, then it is obvious that this would be a different way of gaining God's favor than Abraham's way, for he simply accepted God's promise.

Let me put it another way. The Jewish laws were our teacher and guide until Christ came to give us right standing with God through faith. But now that Christ has come, we don't need those laws any longer to guard us and lead us to him. For now we are all children of God through faith in Jesus Christ, and we who have been baptized into union with Christ are enveloped by him. We are no longer Jews or Greeks or slaves or free men or even merely men or women, but we are all the same – we are Christians; we are one in Christ Jesus. And now that we are Christ's we are the true descendants of Abraham, and all of God's promises to him belong to us. (Galatians 3:14-18, 24-29 TLB)

As stated above, the Manual says those who accept Christ as Lord and Savior are adopted into the Family of God by way of the promise made to Abraham, and Abraham's seed. When Abraham was promised in the agreement with God that he would be the father of many nations, thru Christ the nation of Gentiles and Jews could come under the agreement made to Abraham by way of the Seed, Jesus Christ. These are the ones who accept Christ and His blood as the legal tender offered and given as consideration for the agreement.

What a beautiful exchange! In any agreement or covenant, there must be a mutual giving. A simple example of the agreement-exchange necessity can be found in the agreement, contract, between the buyer and seller of an automobile. The seller and buyer agree to an exchange of money or goods in return for an automobile. The seller may exchange his pretty new red sport's car for the buyer's beautiful green photos of dead presidents.

The beautiful exchange I mentioned above happened after a spiritual vision of the New Covenant (agreement). When I review the

THE NEW COVENANT

spiritual perspective, I see the earthly buying and selling as a representation of the true spiritual exchange. I see God the Father gave His son to the world. The Son (Jesus) gave his life for the world. What God is offering as consideration in his agreement is his only begotten Son. The person who partakes in the agreement receives the offer to become a child of God. Then, because the Son is offered back to God, God the Holy Spirit comes to live inside you to help you keep the agreement.

However, if the partaker in the agreement, now known as a child of God, falls short in meeting the provisions of the agreement, then the Christian will confess the failure and ask the Father to forgive the failure. The forgiveness will be granted because of the forgiveness on the deposit with God through Christ, stored up in the Christian's name.

> If we say that we have no sin, we are only fooling ourselves, and refusing to accept the truth. But if we confess our sins to him, he can be depended on to forgive us and to cleanse us from every wrong. [And it is perfectly proper for God to do this for us because Christ died to wash away our sins.] (I John 1:8-9 TLB)

I'm sure we all have been approached by some individual, whether it was at an airport or a street corner, who gave to us a small piece of paper that spoke of being saved and experiencing salvation. In the religious world the small pieces of paper, in whatever form, are called tracts. These tracts say that to be saved is as simple as ABC.

The "A" stands for *"admit"* that you are a sinner and have need of Jesus Christ as your personal savior:

> For all have sinned and come short of the glory of God. (Romans 3:23)

The "B" stands for *"believe"* in Jesus Christ to be saved.

> Believe on the Lord Jesus Christ and thou shalt be saved. (Acts 16:31)

The "C" stands for *"confess"* that the Son of God, Jesus Christ, is your personal savior.

> For with the heart man believeth unto righteousness; and with the mouth confession is made unto salvation. (Romans 10:10)

"THE" DIET FOR YOUR MIND TO HELP YOU FIND THE TRUTH THAT WILL SET YOU FREE

In conjunction with the above view that being saved is as simple as A,B, and C, we could also consider the following.

The "A" stands for "accept" and "acknowledge." Accept Jesus Christ as your savior:

> But although he made the world, the world didn't recognize him when he came. Even in his own land and among his own people, the Jews, he was not accepted. Only a few would welcome him. But to all who received him, he gave the right to become children of God. All they needed to do was to trust him to save them. All those who believe this are reborn – not a physical rebirth resulting from human passion or plan – but from the will of God. (St. John 1:10-13 TLB)

> For God sent not his Son into the world to condemn the world; but that the world through him might be saved. (St John 3:17)

> For whosoever shall call upon the name of the Lord shall be saved. (Romans 10:13)

And "acknowledge" Jesus as God in the flesh:

> Before anything else existed, there was Christ, with God. He has always been alive and is himself God. (St. John 1:1-2 TLB)

The "B" stands for "believe." Believe that Jesus Christ is God appearing in the flesh and is the only begotten Son of God.

> And Christ became a human being and lived here on earth among us and was full of forgiveness and truth. And some of us have seen his glory – the glory of the only [begotten] Son of the heavenly Father! (St. John 1:14 TLB)

The "C" stands for "confess" your sins and believe that Jesus died for your sins and made it possible for you to live as a child of God.

> If we say that we have no sin, we are only fooling ourselves, and refusing to accept the truth. But if we confess ours sins to him, he can be depended on to forgive us and to cleanse us from every wrong. [And it

THE NEW COVENANT

is perfectly proper for God to do this for us because Christ died to wash away our sins.] (1 John 1:8-9 TLB)

Whether we take either of these approaches to being born-again, we have to agree that the essential element is Jesus. We realize that the natural self will not and cannot obey the Spirit. Therefore, our natural birth, our birth via our natural parents, allows us only to have a diet of the natural. However, since we are spirit, we need to understand the spiritual. The spiritual can only be understood through being born-again: being born of the spirit. So, after this Holy understanding, we seek to be born-again. This seeking of the new birth is the result of realizing that sin is in our nature. There is no way that the natural can avoid sin or be forgiven for it. The way, the truth and the life are only thru Jesus.

Thus, we admit that we are sinners. We believe that the Lord Jesus Christ died for our sins and he will forgive us of our sins. Next, we will confess that Jesus is God in the flesh and He is our personal savior. Then the Holy Spirit will come and live with you to aid you in your walk in the Spirit. Now you are born-again, born a second time, born of the Spirit.

In conclusion we must have a very good "holy understanding" of the new birth. The new birth is rooted in faith. At first there may not be physical evidence of the change. However, this does not discredit the new birth. As you will read below, faith is the belief in the unseen when there is no evidence seen. So, if you don't get the shouting blues, or some other emotional outburst, don't be overly concerned. As natural births vary, so do spiritual births. There may be weeping or laughter on a natural birth, when a child is born. There may or may not be a similar response to a spiritual birth. The key is faith.

THE CHRISTIAN TRINITY:
(THE FRUIT OF THE SPIRIT)
FAITH, HOPE AND LOVE
1. FAITH

The above sounds so easy. We can accept and acknowledge that Jesus is God in the flesh, believe that God in the flesh (Jesus) came to show humanity the way, the truth and the life, confess our sins to God and believe God will forgive us of our sins in the name of Jesus and that the living soul will live in the bosom of Abraham and in the presence of God for eternity.

What else is needed? You may say there has to be more to the soul being saved than living in the presence of God. The answer is nothing else is needed. The ingredients of accepting, believing and confessing, as set out above, are all that is needed. However, the ingredients must be prepared in a bowl of "faith" "hope" and "love."

> And those whose faith has made them good in God's sight must live by faith, trusting him in everything. Otherwise, if they shrink back, God will have no pleasure in them.
>
> But we have never turned our backs on God and sealed our fate. No, our faith in him assures our souls' salvation. (Hebrews 10:38-39 TLB)
>
> What is faith? It is the confident assurance that something we want is going to happen. It is the certainty that what we hope for is waiting for us, even though we cannot see it up ahead. Men of God in days of old were famous for their faith. By faith – by believing God – we know that the world and the stars - in fact, all things - were made at God's command; and they were all made from things that can't be seen.
>
> These men of faith I have mentioned died without ever receiving all that God had promised them; but they saw it all awaiting them on ahead and were glad, for they agreed that this earth was not their real home but that they were just strangers visiting down here.

THE CHRISTIAN TRINITY: (THE FRUIT OF THE SPIRIT)

And quite obviously when they talked like that, they were looking forward to their real home in heaven.

If they had wanted to, they could have gone back to the good things of this world. But they didn't want to. They were living for heaven. And now God is not ashamed to be called their God, for he has made a heavenly city for them. (Hebrews 11:1-3, 13-16 TLB)

Now that we know what faith is, how do we get faith?

So then faith cometh by hearing, and hearing by the word of God. (Romans 10:17)

Yet faith comes from listening to this Good News – the Good News about Christ. (Romans 10:17 TLB)

The above statement from the Manual simply says that if one is to have or gain faith, one must find the hope and belief of things to come by and through the Word of God. To put it another way, one must hear about the words in the Manual. After one has heard of the Manual, one must consult and read the Manual. After consulting and reading the Manual, one must believe the words in the Manual. After one has come to believe the words in the Manual, which is only accomplished by first being born-again, one will have faith.

To give an explanation in terms of physical observance, the following could be used to understand the faith.

A friend, LaQuisa invites you to her church. While experiencing the services, you hear the preacher telling you about The Father, Son and Holy Spirit. (You have just heard.)

Thus, since you have heard the Word, something within you (the Spirit of God) comes alive and you begin to believe the Word you heard. (You have begun to believe.)

Next, you find yourself seeking to follow what the Word says. You begin to love thy neighbor as thy self, and to love the Lord with all your heart, mind and soul. Your vision of life on earth is seen as temporal and you are constantly ignoring the five senses and placing them under the sixth sense. Therefore, since you are seeking first the kingdom of God, and his will, you trust God to be true to his word; God will supply all your earthly need from his riches in glory, because of what Christ Jesus has done for us.

"THE" DIET FOR YOUR MIND TO HELP YOU FIND THE TRUTH THAT WILL SET YOU FREE

I have found that when God leads us to faith, he places knowledge into our PCS. You see faith is only gained through knowledge and experience. Thus, faith, unlike hope, must be preceded with knowledge. This knowledge will be supported by an experience. An example of this point can be seen from the scriptures above. However, to further illustrate, the need for knowledge and experience can be seen in a simple explanation.

Remember that according to the above definition, faith is the assurance that something we want is going to happen. When we visit a place where seating is required – we could use the theater as an example – we go to a seat and sit down. If you reach out to examine the chair, it is only to locate the chair in the darkness of the theater. Anyway, you locate the seat and sit. Why would you enter a place where you have not gone before, sit in a seat you have not sat in before without making an extensive examination of the chair? I'll tell you why. The reason you sat in the seat without examining it is that you have heard about or seen a chair before. From experience, you have the knowledge that chairs are made to sit in.

Furthermore, you believed that the chair would do what it is supposed to do; it would allow you to sit in it. So, you trusted or had faith that the thing you wanted – to sit in chair – would happen. Now this was not based upon a wish or on pulling a magical result from the air. Rather, your trust and faith were based upon knowledge – chairs are made to sit in – and the experience of sitting in a chair.

This is the way it is when walking in the Spirit of God. God, from the time of your second birth, will be with you guiding you in experiences so you will gain knowledge to trust and have faith in him. Thus, a relationship is formed by faith, the relationship of friend to friend and child to father (you to God).

2. HOPE

The Webster Dictionary defines hope as the cherishing of a desire with the expectation of its fulfillment. To hope is to long for something with the expectation of obtaining it. Hope is a desire accompanied by the expectation of or belief in its fulfillment.

THE CHRISTIAN TRINITY: (THE FRUIT OF THE SPIRIT)

Again, we must distinguish between the world or the natural and the spiritual. Hope, like the air humanity breathes, is used by all humanity. However, there is a difference between the Christian and non-Christian's faith and hope. The difference is that the non-Christian's faith is usually rooted in a resume, the person's experiences and knowledge of the natural. So, the non-Christian has hope in self. The Christian's faith is rooted in experiences and knowledge of God as well as the resume.

When hope and faith are viewed, they appear to be the same. However, there is a difference between the two. They are not the opposite of one another; rather they are very close relatives.

As mentioned above, to have faith one has to have knowledge and experience. With hope, there is knowledge and experience, and knowledge and experience are called faith. Therefore, hope, when rooted in the word of God, is the result of experience and knowledge, (faith). So faith, experiences and knowledge, is what hope is based upon.

Let's observe faith and hope in action. I will appear at Please Hire Me, Inc. on Monday seeking a job. I will go in hope. When I appear, I have the desire and expectation that I will be hired.

Instead of appearing only with the hope, desire and expectation of being hired, I also appear with faith. By appearing with hope and faith, I believe that God has led me to Please Hire Me, Inc. Furthermore, I am trusting not only in my resume but in God. If the job is the best thing for me, then, I will get the job.

If I am not hired and I only have hope, I will leave with disappointment. My desire and expectation were not fulfilled. If I have faith, but I'm not hired, then I will leave not with disappointment but rather in the hope of another appointment. You see, faith in God means having a relationship with God. However, hope without faith in God, means I am being positively minded. With hope, several non-hires will only result in several disappointments. With faith, after several non-hires I can keep hope alive and view the non-hires only as an indication that I have not yet understood the message from God.

Where in the Manual would I find the substance of what I hoped for – the confident assurance that something I want was going to

"THE" DIET FOR YOUR MIND TO HELP YOU FIND THE TRUTH THAT WILL SET YOU FREE

happen? Where can I find the certainty that what I hope for is waiting for me, even though I can't see it up ahead?

Yes, I have read all of Chapter Eleven of Hebrews in the Manual. Therein, I read how by faith the elders obtained a good report. Furthermore, I have read in the Living Bible at Hebrews Chapter Eleven that, "Men of God in days of old were famous for their faith." Some of the men mentioned were Abel, Enoch, Noah and Abraham. These men of old were found in the Old Testament. Now I know God's word is the same yesterday, today and evermore, but where in the New Testament, under which I am presently living, can I find God speaking to me. Thus, by His word I can find the word (faith) that will be my anchor to build my hope upon.

As I was seeking, God helped me to find an anchor. I will not say that this is the only anchor, for all of God's word should be an anchor. Anyway, I was led to the Book of Romans and the Eighth Chapter. Whenever I am in doubt, lacking faith and therefore also lacking hope in God, I turn to this chapter in the Manual and focus on the following verses:

> So there is now no condemnation awaiting those who belong to Christ Jesus. For the power of the life-giving Spirit – and this power is mine through Christ Jesus – has freed me from the vicious circle of sin and death. We aren't saved by knowing the commandments of God, because we can't and don't keep them, but God put into effect a different plan to save us. He sent his own son in a human body like ours – except that ours are sinful – and destroyed sin's control over us by giving himself as a sacrifice for our sins. (Roman 8:1-3 TLB)
>
> Yet, even though Christ lives within you, your body will die because of sin, but your spirit will live, for Christ has pardoned it. And if the Spirit of God, who raised up Jesus from the dead, lives in you, he will make your dying bodies live again after you die, by means of this same Holy Spirit living within you. (Romans 8:10-11 TLB)

THE CHRISTIAN TRINITY: (THE FRUIT OF THE SPIRIT)

> We are saved by trusting. And trusting means looking forward to getting something we don't yet have – for a man who already has something doesn't need to hope and trust that he will get it. But if we must keep trusting God for something that hasn't happened yet, it teaches us to wait patiently and confidently. (Romans 8:24-25 TLB)

> But if we hope for that we see not, then do we with patience wait for it. (Romans 8:25)

> And we know that all that happens to us is working for our good if we love God and are fitting into his plans.

> What can we ever say to such wonderful things as these? If God is on our side, who can be against us? Since he did not spare even his son for us but gave him up for us all, won't he also surely give us everything else? (Romans 8:28,31-32 TLB)

RELATIONSHIPS:
(THE FAMILY, THE CHURCH)

Before we go to the third part of the Christian Trinity, love, we must understand what God is seeking in having a person born-again, as well as His purpose with man (humanity).

When we began with the first book of the Manual (the Holy Bible), we learned that God created man. God created man to have dominion (control) over the earth, the earth that was also created by God. Man was God's most cherished creation.

> No, for in the book of Psalms David says to God, "What is mere man that you are so concerned about him? And who is this Son of Man you honor so highly? For though you made him lower than the angels for a little while, now you have crowned him with glory and honor. And you have put him in complete charge of everything there is. Nothing is left out."

We have not seen all of this take place, but we do see Jesus – who for a while was a little lower than the angels – crowned now by God with glory and honor because he suffered death for us. Yes, because of God's great kindness, Jesus tasted death for everyone in all the world. And it was right and proper that God, who made everything for his own glory, should allow Jesus to suffer, for in doing this he was bringing vast multitudes of God's people to heaven; for his suffering made Jesus a perfect Leader, one fit to bring them into their salvation.

We who have been made holy by Jesus, now have the same Father he has. This is why Jesus is not ashamed to call us his brothers. For he said in the book of Psalms, "I will talk to my brothers about God my father, and together we will sing his praises." At another time he said, "I will put my trust in God along with my brothers." And at still another time, "See, here am I and the children God gave me." (Hebrews 2:6-13 TLB)

We now can see that God, the Father, wants man and woman to be as children, and therefore look to Him as a Father. In other words, God wants a family.

We have mentioned above before Jesus' coming, in God's sight there were two nations of people. The two nations were the Jews, the nation God had set aside for all of the others to see as an example of His children, and all other peoples, who were known as Gentiles. Thus, His family would have been called the Jews or Israelites.

In Webster's, we will find several definitions of the family. Webster's says the family is a group of individuals living under one roof and usually under one head, a household. Family can also be a group of people united by certain convictions or a common affiliation, a fellowship.

The household where there is fellowship of people united in certain convictions as to the divinity of Jesus (the family) is called the "church." The church is not an organization or a building, but an organism – the body of Christ.

THE CHRISTIAN TRINITY: (THE FRUIT OF THE SPIRIT)

With the church came three types of peoples: the Gentiles, the Jews and the church people, Christians. God the Son, Jesus, is the head of the Church here on earth. Thus, it could be said that Jesus is head of the Kingdom of heaven. Then when He delivers the church up to God the Father, you'll find God the Father as the head of the church (the family) in the Kingdom of God. As head of the household, the Kingdom of God, He wants the group of people who are united in certain convictions and common affiliation to have fellowship through the blood of God the Son (Jesus). Thus, through Jesus comes the new birth by the Holy Spirit and the adoption into the family of God. Therefore, as an adoptive child, the child is entitled to all the same rights as the biological child. The adoptive child, like the biological child, has the right to inherit as an heir, or joint-heir. All are God's children – the biological child of God, Jesus, and all that accept Jesus as the "only begotten child" of God the Father.

> And if children, then heirs: heirs of God, and joint-heirs with Christ. (Romans 8:17 TLB)

We can see where Jesus, God the Son, wants man to be a brother. (See Hebrews 2:13 above)

Finally, we can see that God, the Holy Spirit, wants man to be a dwelling place.

> Haven't you yet learned that your body is the home of the Holy Spirit God gave you, and that he lives within you? Your own body does not belong to you. (1 Corinthians 6:19 TLB)

A review of God the Father wanting humanity to see him as a father, of Jesus wanting siblings, and of the Holy Spirit wanting a home, shows a desire for intimacy, a family, or in other words, a relationship – the relationship between God and man, which existed in the Garden of Eden before the eating of the forbidden fruit. A relationship by and through the Spirit ended when man ate the forbidden fruit, thereby allowing a spirit contrary to the Spirit of God to come and live in man. This contrary spirit brought dysfunction to the family of God and to the family of humanity.

As stated before, to overcome this contrary spirit, man had to be born-again. Thus, after the new birth, man had access to his original state of the Holy Spirit living inside of man to combat the contrary spirit.

The above scriptures show how the Holy Trinity (The Father, Son, and Holy Spirit) worked together, and are working together, for the family relationship between God and humanity. The Father sent the Son, the Son gave his life and the Holy Spirit works to help the born again person become more like Christ.

> For all who are led by the Spirit of God are sons of God. And so we should not be like cringing fearful slaves, but we should behave like God's very own children, adopted into the bosom of his family, and calling to him, "Father, Father." For his Holy Spirit speaks to us deep in our hearts, and tells us that we are his children, we will share his treasures – for all God gives to his Son Jesus is now ours too. But if we are to share in his glory, we must also share his suffering. (Romans 8:14-17 TLB)

This relationship, between God and humanity, is based upon faith. This is the faith that since God didn't spare his only begotten Son, but delivered him up for us all, He will, with Jesus, give us everything. Furthermore, this faith is supported by the covenants, the Abrahamic and New Covenants. The Abrahamic Covenant was a covenant between God and Abram (Abraham), the Jewish nation, and the New Covenant was between God and whoever will accept Jesus as Lord and Savior.

The relationship also contains hope – the expectation that what the Manual says will come to be.

However, in the Christian Trinity, greater than faith, and hope, is the element of the relationship called love – the love of a parent for the child, God the heavenly Father for His children. The example of love by the Father is to be followed by His children with love toward one another.

> This is my commandment, That ye love one another, as I have loved you. (Saint John 15:12)

THE CHRISTIAN TRINITY: (THE FRUIT OF THE SPIRIT)

3. LOVE
(DESSERT)

If I had the gift of being able to speak in other languages without learning them, and could speak in every language there is in all heaven and earth, but didn't love others, I would only be making noise.

If I had the gift of prophecy and knew all about what is going to happen in the future, knew everything about everything, but didn't love others, what good would it do? Even if I had the gift of faith so that I could speak to a mountain and make it move, I would still be worth nothing at all without love. If I gave everything I have to poor people, and if I were burned alive for preaching the Gospel but didn't love others, it would be of no value whatever.

Love is very patient and kind, never jealous or envious, never boastful or proud, never haughty or selfish or rude. Love does not demand its own way. It is not irritable or touchy. It does not hold grudges and will hardly even notice when others do it wrong.

It is never glad about injustice, but rejoices whenever truth wins out. If you love someone you will be loyal to him no matter what the cost. You will always believe in him, always expect the best of him, and always stand your ground in defending him.

All the special gifts and powers from God will someday come to an end, but love goes on forever. Someday prophecy, and speaking in unknown languages, and special knowledge – these gifts will disappear.

Now we know so little, even with our special gifts, and the preaching of those most gifted is still so poor. But when we have been made perfect and complete, then the need for these inadequate gifts will come to an end, and they will disappear.

"THE" DIET FOR YOUR MIND TO HELP YOU FIND THE TRUTH THAT WILL SET YOU FREE

It's like this: when I was a child I spoke and thought and reasoned as a child does. But when I became a man my thoughts grew far beyond those of my childhood, and now I have put away the childish things. In the same way we can see and understand only a little about God now, as if we were peering at his reflection in a poor mirror; but someday we are going to see him in his completeness, face to face. Now all that I know is hazy and blurred, but then I will see everything clearly as God sees into my heart right now.

There are three things that remain – faith, hope, and love – and the greatest of these is love. (1 Corinthians 13, TLB)

LOVE AND RELATIONSHIPS[1]

Some time ago, I was invited to sit on a panel with others to discuss love and relationships. After listening to the discussion, two observations were made. First, I observed that most individuals present were trying to understand love from a physical perspective. This gnosis of love has led many to a bitter and fearful approach to relationships. However, I believe once you have read the following presentation, understood the secrets contained within, and applied the principles to your life, you will have a better approach to understanding love and relationships.

As a panel member, when I asked for a definition of love, the response was: "There is no one definition of love. If you ask around in this setting, as with the world, you will get a different answer from each of us." Thus, my second observation was the recognition of the truth of the statement. Even in the church, the light of the world, we may know the necessity and importance of love. However, when it comes to understanding what love is, we are inclined to look to the physical or to give definitions rooted in the physical. Hence, the purpose of this writing is to address these observations.

After several years of research, prayer, and meditation, I have learned that God is love and God is a spirit. Therefore, to define love, to understand love – even physical (Eros) love – the approach has to begin in, of, and through the Spirit.

A definition of love, which I believe to be a definitive one, will be given in an attempt to establish a standard. Some time ago, a foot of an item was measured according to the foot, arm, or some other part of the purchaser's anatomy. In the effort to eliminate discrepancies (everybody having his/her own measurement of what was a foot) a standard (twelve inches) was established. Hence, the world came to agreement on the measure of a foot.

Therefore, a definition, which was arrived at through the spirit according to God's Holy Word, is introduced to aid our striving to come to agreement. This will eliminate the differences between our definitions.

"THE" DIET FOR YOUR MIND TO HELP YOU FIND THE TRUTH THAT WILL SET YOU FREE

In the effort to come to agreement, the proposed definition is repeated, against the editor's objections, throughout these pages. Inasmuch as the main purpose of this presentation is to inform, as opposed to entertain, I deem the repetition necessary.

INTRODUCTION TO THE DESSERT

There are many things we experience each day that we do not totally understand. Nevertheless, I have come to recognize two planes (spheres) of existence:
>The physical (tangible), and
>The spiritual (intangible).

Aerodynamics may explain the principles involved in the ability of an airplane or even a bird to fly. However, what creates or enforces these principles within a logical or physical sphere cannot be explained. Thus, the spiritual realm must be entered. Once we enter the spiritual or cosmic spheres, human understanding becomes very limited.

The above planes are mentioned because they will be referred to throughout this writing. An attempt is being made to become of one accord, an agreement, and thereby establish a common base for understanding and communicating the forthcoming. Furthermore, some will not accept the two planes mentioned because of lack of belief or lack of experience of the spiritual. The physical existence – that which can be seen – is readily accepted. However, the spiritual existence – that which cannot be seen with the human eye – will be denied. Although, you may not be a believer in a supreme being – the spiritual – you have to accept that there are things that are seen and unseen. This writing is primarily based in and on the unseen – the spiritual – while sometimes using the seen – the physical – secondarily.

Man and woman, since Adam and Eve, have sought to understand what love is. They sang about it and wrote poems about it. All this was done in the search for love and the expression of what love is. You hold in your hand one more of humanity's attempts to understanding the meaning of love.

There was a time in my life when I thought nothing would be more pleasing than the physical niceties of this world. Let me say, without going into the facts of my conversion, I finally recognized that though the physical was present, peace, joy and happiness were not. Therefore, I began to think, there had to be another answer. Then

"THE" DIET FOR YOUR MIND TO HELP YOU FIND THE TRUTH THAT WILL SET YOU FREE

I remembered my parents' teaching, and pastors' preaching, about a God of Spirit. I made a decision. I believe the Holy Spirit led me, to, "Seek…first the kingdom of God." In other words, I decided to look into the spiritual.

> But seek ye first the kingdom of God, and his righteousness; and all these things shall be added unto you. (St. Matthew 6:33)

Only by a change from self-consciousness, which began with a change of mind, could I have gained what I will share. The change of mind came by way of a change of diet for my mind, a diet that led to the God-consciousness. With growth in the Spirit, my mind changed from thoughts rooted in world-consciousness, to find a greater self. After the self was born again, I found the way, the truth and the life. The way was the creator's way; after all, I am a creation and the creator knows what's best for His creation.

The truth is the truth of the creator that made me free. The life is the life of truth, and the way is the creator's way of life, which entails living life more abundantly. In other words, I let Jesus into my mind and heart. I became born again and placed my mind on a diet.

My natural birth (first birth) was of the physical and my mind pursued the things of the flesh. When I let Jesus into my mind, He also entered my heart. Thus, I stopped seeking conformity to this world and began a transformation by the renewing of my mind. This renewing of my mind has caused my thoughts to be not after things of the flesh, but rather, thinking and seeking the things of the Spirit.

> And be not conformed to this world: but be ye transformed by the renewing of your mind, that ye may prove what is that good, and acceptable, and perfect, will of God. (Romans 12:2)

> That the righteousness of the law might be fulfilled in us, who walk not after the flesh, but after the spirit. For they that are after the flesh do mind the things of the flesh; but they that are after the spirit the things of the spirit. (Romans 8:4-5)

I still don't know everything, but I have found a key to everything. I have found the key to have life more abundantly, to understand life. To truly live life is to come to accept that all

INTRODUCTION TO THE DESSERT

knowledge of life is rooted in the spiritual. The tangible, the physical, the seen, is not always what it appears to be. The clichés "All that glitters isn't gold," "You can't judge a book by its cover" and "Believe half of what you see" are common expressions and manifestations. There is fool's gold. Books can have surprising contents and demonic hypnotists do and will exist. However, when the mind, body and the soul are recording their information under the guidance of the Holy Spirit, the sixth sense, then the true nature of what is being received is exposed for what it is in truth.

This is clearly understood when one reads about the life of Jesus. The nature of tricky questions was readily understood by Him, simply because He began His examination of the source by way of the Spirit. Regardless, of whether He was approached as "Rabbi," a person to receive respect, or "blasphemer," a despised person, He listened not to the name, but to the source of the names. (Please read St. Matthew 9:1-8, 12:22-37, and St. John 8:1-11)

This writer has nothing against the physical. But, in love, if the physical is used as the lowest common denominator (LCD), then we will continue to have a high rate of divorces and numerous confused persons. Therefore, let's take another approach to love before we start asking the question, "What's love got to do with it?" as in the popular song.

I have also discovered, from my experiences, that the new approach will start with self. Before you find reflections of others in these few words, first, find the reflections of yourself. Please be aware that your true self goes beyond your physical (seen) body (flesh). It's the spiritual self, the unseen, often neglected self that you are to discover. Then when you have allowed this new self to grow, faith, hope and love will lie within your grasp. As the old Negro Spiritual says, "No more weeping and wailing," for indeed you would have come to live with God – God, the Creator, the Redeemer, the Love, the Omnipotent, the Everlasting, the Alpha and Omega, the Creator of you, me and all. Inasmuch as God created you, and the creator always knows what's best for the creation, God (the Creator) knows what's best for you. When you are in touch with the Creator's specification (God's will), according to His Manual (God's word), He'll make you well when you are ill. He is there to give you peace when you are depressed; and He's there to comfort you when you're in need of a friend. All is done in the name of love. You will come to understand yourself and God, through Jesus Christ. Thus, you are to proceed from this point *seeking* – and ye shall find – *asking* – and it will be given unto you – *knocking* at the door of "spiritual knowledge" – and the truth will be opened unto you. He who has ears, let him hear with understanding.

This writer, although realizing that the root of love, the foundation of understanding love, if found in the spiritual, will not and cannot deny eros (the physical, erotic), which is also a form of love. Furthermore, a clear understanding of love is elusive and escapes understanding in the spiritual as well as the physical. There are some things that we are not able to understand one hundred percent. Suppose a friend whom you had not heard from in weeks, months or years called you and before the call, maybe several days before, this friend had been constantly on your mind. Or, why is it that when you were away from home attending college, your mother would call and without your telling her a thing, she already knew when something was wrong?

We could go on endlessly with examples of experiences that we don't completely understand. And to be honest with you, we humans, even with our space programs, even with our medical programs and heart transplants, surrogate mothers and so on, do not completely understand everything. Galileo's study of the stars was incomplete. Einstein's theories of relativity and mathematical equations were known only in part. Edison could go only so far with his electrical experiments. Thus, it will suffice to say that these men – our geniuses –knew only in part, understood only in part. It's as if the whole denies any one person or thing knowledge of the whole. The Creator denies the creation full understanding, and thereby presents the necessity for a relationship, an interaction of the parties – God and humanity – rooted in faith. Hence, to understand the whole is important, but I thank God for seeing and understanding in part the constant unfolding of the truth – the truth that will set me free.

The two covenants of God mentioned above show the revelation of God in part. First in the Old Testament, we had God through His prophets working with the people through the Law. In the New

INTRODUCTION TO THE DESSERT

Testament, we have the Son, teaching and preaching love: love God, love thy neighbor and love thy enemy (through grace). Thereby, we move from the law to grace. Next, the Holy Spirit was given by Jesus to lead us into wisdom and knowledge. However, as Paul said in I Corinthians 13, knowledge will pass away, but love will always be. Do you know why? Because God is love; God is the Alpha and Omega. God always was and always will be.

One of the reasons we fail to understand completely what has been revealed is that most of us wish to go into the twelfth grade from the first grade. We do not understand the second through eleventh but wish to be in the twelfth. We have overlooked the minor and sought the major revelations. However, when we examine the revelations of God, we could say they were done one day, one month, one year or one decade at a time. So what is known now in the Twenty-First-Century was begun at creation.

There is no need at this time to explore the physical aspect of love. Since our understanding is only in part, and this writer believes that what has been revealed in the spiritual is the first and most important part of love to learn. The physical will be left to be experienced after learning of the spiritual. One caveat I will leave with you: henceforth, be as sure as possible that any and all of your future actions of love are rooted in the spiritual, which gives the truth that will make you free to experience true love, and even better, erotic love.

"THE" DIET FOR YOUR MIND TO HELP YOU FIND THE TRUTH THAT WILL SET YOU FREE

WHAT IS LOVE?

Probably more books have been written and more songs have been sung about love than any other subject. Love has been explored on the levels of imaginary love in fiction, classical love in literature, and actual love in true love stories.

Love has been found in the "how to" books. Then, after these and other areas were exhausted, came writings on how to make love. Yet in the Twenty-First-Century, years after nineteen eighty-four (1984) when Tina Turner asked, *What's Love Got to Do With It?*, years after "free love," the hippies and the flower children of the 1960s and the "Do Your Own Thing" of the 1970s, we hear the question, "What is love?"

These and other years will be mentioned because I can identify with experiencing the observation of how humanity has sought to find and understand love. From my observing humanity during these years I have heard the question and seen the pursuit of the answer to "what is love?" I observed the pursuit and the experiences of the 1960s' "free love" and the 1970s' "Do Your Own Thing" to be superficial. Thus the experiences, being superficial or lacking of the Spirit, had no roots in themselves.

Maybe we can gain a better understanding of why I believe the experiences and seeking were superficial through scripture. I am reminded of the scripture:

> The farmer I talked about is anyone who brings God's message to others, trying to plant good seed within their lives. The hard pathway, where some of the seed fell, represents the hard hearts of some of those who hear God's message; Satan comes at once to try to make them forget it. The rocky soil represents the hearts of those who hear the message with joy, but like young plants in such soil, their roots don't go very deep, and though at first they get along fine, as soon as persecution begins they wilt. The thorny ground represents the hearts of people who listen to the good news and receive it, but all too quickly the attractions

WHAT IS LOVE?

of this world and the delights of wealth, and the search for success and lure of nice things come in and crowd out God's message in their hearts, so that no crop is produced. But the good soil represents the hearts of those who truly accept God's message and produce a plentiful harvest for God – thirty, sixty, or even a hundred times as much as was planned in their hearts." (St. Mark 4: 14-20 TLB)

Wherefore by their fruits ye shall know them. (St. Matthew 7:20)

I would characterize, by observing its fruit, our present position in reference to truly understanding love, as bearing fruit of the third seed. Below, we can get a visual understanding of where we are in knowledge about love. (Note that understanding love has reference to the masses.)

1st Seed	Top of Ground –A Glance- (Taken Away Before Rooting)	Before 1960

2nd Seed	Shallow Ground – A Taste- (Short Endurance, Love Everybody, In The Physical, Free Love)	1960
3rd Seed	Thistles Ground – A Knowledge – (But, Desires the Physical over the Spiritual)	70s – 80s – and 90s

Thus, having experienced only the physical (superficial) and not having gained total understanding, which is only attainable at the fourth seed level, the world throws up its hands and cries out, "What's

"THE" DIET FOR YOUR MIND TO HELP YOU FIND THE TRUTH THAT WILL SET YOU FREE

love got to do with it?" "I can't find it, so why do I need it?" and "Anyway, what is love?"

Hence, when one observes the sales of *I Want To Know What Love Is* by the Foreigners and The New Jersey Mass Choir[1], and Ms. Tina Turner's recording of *What's Love Got To Do With It?*[2] one notices that most individuals were still asking the same questions in the '80s.

In the '90s, humanity sought a physically sound body, recognizing the need to keep the physical in shape. Next, humanity found a hard drive and fell in love with technology and through technology continued to seek love.

The cellular, PC, and DVD, to name a few, are what humanity, with a physical understanding of love, fall in love with and use to find love. However, since there was no diet for the mind and no seeking or being under the control of the Spirit, when the cellular was used, world-consciousness responded. The chat room on the PC only reminded the chatter that the other chatters were still tuned in to the physical. Finally, the DVD only changed the means of receiving what, for the most part, was created with a worldly understanding.

I must say that loving, in this case loving technology, and finding love, are spiritually sound principles. This is evidenced in loving Jesus and Jesus loving you. Thus, from this love of Jesus comes the love of the Father and the Holy Spirit. However, this only works from a fourth seed perspective, the good ground. Love through the physical, even in the absence of sexual activity, can only produce a glance of spiritual love.

The recording artists are asking musically what all at one time or another have asked and are hoping to find. There could be an answer, if only the world would dry its eyes and look beneath the superficial (physical) and find the root (the spirit) of love. Maybe the world is looking to find the KFC's Colonel at McDonalds and Mr. Goodwrench at Ford. The search could be for the right thing but it's definitely in the wrong place, and we have seen in scripture (spirit) what will be the results when the seed is correct but the soil is not the right or good ground. Note that the fourth seed was the seed that produced and it was planted in the right place (ground).

WHAT IS LOVE?

Since the twentieth century's superficial experiences have not taught us the truth about love, since we have tried the physical and are still confused, then why not try another basis for understanding love, the best basis, which is the spiritual?

Now, we must come to an understanding. If after reading this far, you are still a non-believer in the Holy Bible, and God through Jesus Christ, and you desire to arrive at an honest answer to what love is, you must read the following, which is supported with scripture and spiritual knowledge. This is what we Christians (believers) do. We realize that there is order and consistency; that can be seen in everyday experiences.

The existence of order and consistency has brought us to the conclusion that there is a Supreme Being who is responsible for the same. Therefore, when we Christians cannot find logical or physical evidence to prove or disprove, we walk by faith. We simply define faith as to belief – *when there may not be any logical or any tangible thing to support that belief. Even though we may not have logical or tangible evidence, because of the knowledge and evidence of the one we have faith in, we'll have faith in the unseen.*

> Now faith is the substance of things hoped for, the evidence of things not seen. Through faith we understand that the worlds were framed by the word of God, so that things which are seen were not made of things which do appear. (Hebrews 11:1,3)
>
> (For we walk by faith, not by sight:) (II Corinthians 5:7)

Christians and non-Christians may share similar experiences. However, the response to and recognition of these experiences will probably differ. This is because Christians recognize a power greater than themselves. This power is greater than any power that can be found in the world or the self. They call this power God.

The purpose here is to take notice that in any attempt to fully understand love, we must first understand God; for God is love. *(1John 4:16)* Furthermore, we have to realize that it is impossible to fully comprehend God. However, there are the things which He has manifested for our knowledge and has shown us in the physical that demonstrate Him as a Spirit. A manifestation God has given us is not a clear definition of love, but rather a clear example of love. From this example, we possibly can find a definition or understand a little more about love (God).

Some will say, "Yes, if you believe in 'that stuff,'" referring to the Holy Bible and God of course. Hence, they forget we all believe in some "stuff." We may believe in his/her, or our/their, or your/my stuff, as described above. At least we can all agree that there are some common existences that each believes in. There is the wind. We cannot see it but we can feel it; therefore, we believe in the wind. A tooth may ache and we experience the pain that we cannot see; nevertheless, we believe in the existence of pain.

So, what's wrong with believing in a God we cannot see? We have had countless testimonies that He exists? He is a God of Spirit that cannot be seen in the physical, but has countless physical manifestations that can be seen and experienced. Some of these manifestations are the trees, the birds, the stars, the moon, the sun, the earth, the flowers, and you and I. Finally, let's not forget His manifestation as Jesus, God in the physical.

> Philip said, "Sir, show us the Father and we will be satisfied." Jesus replied, "Don't you even yet know who I am, Philip, even after all this time I have been with you? Anyone who has seen me has seen the Father! So, why are you asking to see him? (St John 14:8-9 TLB)

Furthermore, it is possible for a person to consider himself or herself a Christian and still not understand love. This is possible inasmuch as Jesus accepts us, as we are when we are *saved* or born-again through a new birth (a spiritual birth) in Christ. There may not have been enough time to eliminate all the pre-born-again programming and replace it with God-consciousness programming. So, the eyes and mind are not fully trained – transformed or renewed – and the focus continues to be rooted in the physical.

Then there are the Christians who do not study the Bible to know God. Hence, they don't know God through His word. The results with these types of Christians are the same as with a non-believer: they continue to look in the wrong place for the right thing.

THE DEFINING ELEMENTS OF LOVE
1. GIVING

Yes, God is a Spirit (St. John 4:24). However, knowing our desire to learn of Him, He came in a physical form to help us understand.

> In the beginning was the Word, and the Word was with God, and the Word was God. And the Word was made flesh, and dwelt among us,...(St. John 1:1,14)

Thus in Jesus' coming, we find – as mentioned above – the greatest example of love in the Manual at St. John 3: 16—17:

> For God so loved the world, that He gave His only begotten Son, that whosoever believeth in Him should not perish, but have everlasting life. For God sent not His Son into the world to condemn the world; but that the world through Him might be saved.

> For I delivered unto you first of all that which I also received, how that Christ died for our sins according to the scriptures; (I Corinthians 15:3)

The scriptures state it plainly and clearly. They do not mention love as a weak feeling in the knees, an upset in the stomach, or a pain in the heart. Simply, God loved, so God gave. God gave not because He was forced, coerced or tricked. The giving was because of need – a need for mankind to have a better means of bringing humanity back to God. Since, God so loved that He gave, we can say that the first element of love is giving.

Inasmuch as Jesus is God's love to the world, if we study His behavior we should see love in action. After all, even the most physically rooted mind knows that love is an action word. Arriving at the New Testament, proceeding through Matthew, Mark, Luke and John, we can read divinely inspired recordings of His life style.

Can we find His action of giving and giving freely and unconditionally? Yes, we can. There are numerous recordings of His giving.

He gave the Word of life:

It is the spirit that quickeneth; the flesh profiteth nothing: the words that I speak unto you, they are spirit, and they are life. (St John 6:63), and
Sight to the blind,

And as Jesus passed by, he saw a man which was blind from his birth. And his disciples asked him, saying, Master, who did sin, this man, or his parents, that he was born blind? Jesus answered, Neither hath this man sinned, nor his parents: but that the works of God should be made manifest in him. I must work the works of him that sent me, while it is day: the night cometh, when no man can work. As long as I am in the world, I am the light of the world. When he had thus spoken, he spat on the ground, and he anointed the eyes of the blind man with the clay. And said unto him, Go, wash in the pool of Siloam, (which is by interpretation, Sent.) He went his way therefore, and washed, and came seeing. (St. John 9:1-7) and,
Hearing to the deaf, and speech to the dumb,

And they bring unto him one that was deaf, and had an impediment in his speech; and they beseech him to put his hand upon him. And he took him aside from the multitude, and put his fingers into his ear, and he spit, and touched his tongue; And looking up to heaven, he sighed, and saith unto him, Ephphatha, that is, Be opened.

And straightway his ears were opened, and the string of his tongue was loosed, and he spake plain. (St Mark 7:32-35), and
Legs to the lame and forgiveness of sin,

And he entered into a ship, and passed over, and came into his own city. And, behold, they brought to him a man sick of the palsy, lying on a bed: and Jesus seeing their faith said unto the sick of the palsy; Son, be of good cheer; thy sins be forgiven thee. And behold, certain of the scribes said, within themselves, This man blasphemeth. And Jesus knowing their

THE DEFINING ELEMENTS OF LOVE

thoughts said, Wherefore think ye evil in your hearts? For whether is easier, to say, Thy sins be forgiven thee; or to say, Arise, and walk? But that ye may know that the Son of man hath power on earth to forgive sins, (then saith he to the sick of the palsy,) Arise, take up thy bed, and go unto thine house. And he arose, and departed to his house. (St. Matthew 9:1-7), and

His greatest example of giving was on the cross at Calvary, where He gave His life for the world,

> Then delivered he him therefore unto them to be crucified. And they took Jesus, and led him away. And he bearing his cross went forth into a place called the place of a skull, which is called in the Hebrew Golgotha: where they crucified him, and two other with him, on either side one, and Jesus in the midst. (St. John 19:16-18)

> Wherefore when he cometh into the world, he saith, Sacrifice and offering thou wouldest not, but a body hast thou prepared me: in burnt offerings and sacrifices for sin thou hast no pleasure. Then said I, Lo, I come (in the volume of the book it is written of me,) to do thy will, O God. Above when he said, Sacrifice and offering and burnt-offerings and offering for sin thou wouldest not, neither hadst pleasure therein; which are offered by the law; then said he, Lo, I come to do thy will, O God. He taketh away the first, that he may establish the second. By the which will we are sanctified through the offering of the body of Jesus Christ once and for all. (Hebrews 10:5-10)

> "The Spirit of the Lord is upon me; He has appointed Me to preach Good News to the poor; He has sent Me to heal the brokenhearted and to announce that captives shall be released and the blind shall see, that the downtrodden shall be freed from their oppressors, and that God is ready to give blessings to all who come to Him." (St. Luke 4:18-19 TLB)

"THE" DIET FOR YOUR MIND TO HELP YOU FIND THE TRUTH THAT WILL SET YOU FREE

The above scriptures point out that Jesus' purpose for coming was to give. In the scriptures, He has given us the first step to understanding what love is. Furthermore, I noticed that Jesus gave before He had not received anything for His giving. He knew that even though His life was being given for the world, some would not accept His giving. Thus, He taught when and where there was a need to give, even if the recipient was an enemy, and he believed or knew that the recipient would not repay him.

> "Do you think you deserve credit for merely loving those who love you? Even the godless do that! And if you do good only to those who do you good – is that so wonderful? Even sinners do that much! And if you lend money only to those who can repay you, what good is that? Even the most wicked will lend to their own kind for full return! (St. Luke 6:32-34 TLB)

Before we go further with other scriptures, let those with eyes to see, see, and ears to hear, hear, what the Word is saying. Please see and hear the interchangeable use of the words *love* and *give* in the above quote from scripture.

> "Do you think you deserve credit for merely *giving* to those who *give* to you?
>
> Love your enemies! Do good to them! Lend to them! And don't be concerned about the fact they won't repay. Then your reward from heaven will be very great, and you will truly be acting as sons of God: for He is kind to the unthankful and to those who are very wicked. (St. Luke 6:35TLB)

The same can be done with the above quote from scripture, found at the 35th verse.

> Give to your enemy! Do good to them! Give to them!

I believe that there are eyes that have seen and ears that have heard. The illustration of the interchangeable use of love and give shows that God is saying if we say we love, one action of love is giving.

> Give what you have to anyone who asks you for it; and when things are taken away from you, don't worry

THE DEFINING ELEMENTS OF LOVE

about getting them back. Treat others as you want them to treat you. (St Luke 6:30-31 TLB)

For if you give, you will get! Your gift will return to you in full and overflowing measure, pressed down, shaken together to make room for more, and running over. Whatever measure you use to give – large or small – will be used to measure what is given back to you. (St Luke 6:38)

If I have not said or used the following Latin expression, then either here it is or here it is again, "Res Ipsua Loiqutuer," which translated means "the thing speaks for itself." In this case, it's the word of God that speaks for itself.

2. FORGIVING

Now that we see the life of Jesus, the one given in love, can we see another element to the definition of love?

There was always something that accompanied Jesus' giving; this was forgiving. The above scripture, located at St Matthew 9:1-7, says that when Jesus gave the lame man legs, He also forgave the man of his sins. Thus, the next element of love that we recognize by observing and learning of love through Jesus is forgiving.

When He gave the woman caught in adultery her life – the people who caught the woman were going to stone her to death, but Jesus interceded – He forgave her of her sins (St John 8:1-11). He would heal someone and say, "Thy sins are forgiven." (St Mark 2:1-5) He had forgiveness for Judas, who betrayed Him, Peter, who denied Him, and Thomas, who doubted Him.

And forgive us our debts, as we forgive our debtors. (St. Matthew 6:12)

We recognize these words of forgiving from our Lord's model prayer. They come after the words "Give us this day." However, one of the best examples I can find of His forgiving is His word uttered from the cross. His people and one of His disciples had betrayed him. He was lied on, spat on, beaten on, forced to wear a crown of thorns on His head, forced to carry a cross up to Skull Hill on His back, stripped of His clothing, laughed at and sworn at and he had His feet and hands nailed to the cross. He withstood all the betrayals, disappointments, and shame. Then, turning to the heavenly Father, He said, "Father forgive them." (St. Luke 23:24)

Yes, as He was giving His life for my sins and your sins, He still was able to forgive. He, also had forgiveness for the penitent thief who made the request of Jesus while they both were dying on the cross. (St Like 23:39-43)

Did Jesus say how many times we are to forgive? Yes!

> Take heed to yourselves: If thy brother trespass against thee, rebuke him: and if he repent, forgive him. And if he trespasses against thee seven times in a day, and seven times in a day turn again to thee, saying, I repent; thou shalt forgive him. (St. Luke 17:3-4)

And why should I forgive?

> And when ye stand praying, forgive, if ye have ought against any: that your Father also which is in heaven may forgive you and your trespasses. But if ye do not forgive, neither will your Father which is in heaven forgive your trespasses. (St. Mark 11:25-26)

FORGIVING GOD

I must confess that I had a big problem with using giving, forgiving and understanding as the definition of love when I came to the reciprocal of loving God. Later when we discuss Brotherly and Divine love we will see that love is horizontal and vertical. Horizontal love is person-to-person love, whereas vertical love is person-to-God love.

There was no difficulty in using giving, forgiving, and understanding in person-to-person love. Furthermore, to give to God and seek to understand God was not difficult. However, to forgive God presented some difficulty. After all, who am I to forgive God? Does God need my forgiveness? Furthermore, for the proposed definition of love to be the truth, and we have learned that truth is consistent, the definition used for person-to-person love had to be consistent with the definition of person-to-God love.

THE DEFINING ELEMENTS OF LOVE

Finally, the proposed definition had to be consistent with St. Matthew 22:37-39. In summary, these scriptures say you should love God with all your heart, soul, and mind. This is vertical love (person-to-God love). You should also love your neighbor as much as you love yourself. This is horizontal love (person-to-person love).

Then after a period of time, the Holy Spirit taught me how the definition of love as giving, forgiving and understanding was consistent in person-to-person love and person-to-God love. First, the Holy Spirit reminded me that a mind rooted in the world or self-consciousness cannot understand the Spirit of God. Thus, only a mind that has been renewed, born of the Spirit, that has forsaken the self and world for the Spirit, can understand the Spirit.

In the physical world, the recipient appears to be the blessed one; after all, the gift has enhanced his or her life in some way. But in the Spiritual world, it is the giver, as well as the recipient, who is blessed.

> And I was a constant example to you in helping the poor; for I remember the words of the Lord Jesus: 'It is more blessed to give than to receive.' (Acts 20:35 TLB)

> Then said he also to him that bade him, When thou makest a dinner or a supper, call not thy friends, nor thy brethren, neither thy kinsmen, nor thy rich neighbours; lest they also bid thee again, and a recompence be made thee. But when thou makest a feast, call the poor, the mained, the lame, the blind: And thou shalt be blessed; for they cannot recompense thee: for thy shalt be recompensed at the resurrection of the just. (St. Luke: 14:12-14)

The scripture, mentioned above, at St Luke 6:27-35, tells you to give and lend to even your enemy with no desire to receive from the one you gave to, "And your reward shall be great, and ye shall be the children of the Highest." Thus, as a child of God, the giver through the giving is brought blessings from God. Also, when the giving is prefaced upon not looking for anything in return from the recipient of your giving, you are in essence forgiving the non-payment. Thus, as you forgive the non-payment, you then in fact have given the promissory note to the surety, God the Father. Then, God the Father

"THE" DIET FOR YOUR MIND TO HELP YOU FIND THE TRUTH THAT WILL SET YOU FREE

will either place it in the heart of the recipient to repay, or on the one who promises to repay the promissory note. The Father's payment may be money, which will be several fold, or some other blessing that you may be in need of at the time.

Some time ago, in our bible class studies, we were studying the sixth chapter of St Luke in the Manual. While we were in the discussion of giving, the Holy Spirit presented a live factual situation to see my response. A young man had appeared at the church for money. The pastor was not present, so a member asked that I step out of bible study and speak with the young man. When I returned to the class the students inquired what the young man wanted. I informed them that he said he had recently moved to the area and had worked, but it would be two days, Friday, before he received his first paycheck. He had requested that the church lend him fifteen dollars until Friday. I told the class that I was going to give him the fifteen dollars. I didn't have the fifteen dollars in my pocket but since Thursday was my payday, I would go by a store and write a check for fifteen dollars more than I purchased and give the fifteen dollars to him.

Immediately there were many responses. One student said that often a person would appear at the church with some similar story requesting money. Furthermore, most times the person would request the money to spend on alcohol. They went on to say that I would not get my fifteen dollars back because most of the people who make such requests misuse the money or never repay it. Even if he made the promise to repay, they wouldn't lend this person one red cent.

I reminded the class of our studies: give to those who won't repay, and so on. Finally, the Holy Spirit said to me, and I told the class, "If he doesn't repay me the fifteen dollars, then God will owe me. In fact, I hope he doesn't repay me, so God will owe me. In my effort to help this person, I was doing as Jesus said. I was giving even if a person wouldn't repay. Then God would owe me my reward or repayment. Furthermore, God's source was greater than this person's source."

We have drifted back to giving in my attempt to explain forgiving. The aim here is to see the blessing in giving and also to see the blessing in forgiving. Thus, we give and forgive for our own blessing. Therefore, the forgiving of God is not for God; it's for myself.

The Lord's model prayer says, "Give us this day our daily bread." In the book of James in the Manual, there is the statement, "Ask God and he will give to you." Now, if God knows all, why do you have to ask him for something. The reason is you do it for yourself. When you ask God for something and receive that something, you are programming the mind to depend not on yourself, but on God. So, my forgiveness of God happens not because God needs it. I do it for myself.

"Well," you may say, "When will I need to forgive God?" There are many people who do not attend church or who have turned from the body of Christ, because something has happened and they blamed God, and cannot or would not forgive God.

There may be a child that died at a young age, and the parents are still asking why it died and refusing to forgive God for letting the child die so young.

There is a person who trusted God and believed that his or her spouse would always be there. Well, once he or she left, whether by free will or cessation of life, the person lost the ability to forgive God for allowing the absence of another person.

We could go on and on with examples of persons who have not forgiven God. Remember, when there is no forgiving, of sin or whatever, there is separation. So, the person who does not forgive God is separated from God, and therefore has as their source only what the world and a self-fed mind and heart can provide, which is usually something that destroys the body and soul.

Thus, I forgive God, not because God needs my forgiveness, but because I trust God. I trust God as a friend, a father, and a creator. Therefore, even though I may wish that my younger sister had lived more than a few hours after her birth, I believe that God took her to be with Him and I'll see her one day in heaven. In other words, I may have wanted my sister to be with me, but God wanted her to be with Him. So, I accept God's decision because I trust Him and believe that Father knows best.

"THE" DIET FOR YOUR MIND TO HELP YOU FIND THE TRUTH THAT WILL SET YOU FREE

3. UNDERSTANDING

Then there was one other noticeable behavioral characteristic associated with this child who was born to show us the way, the truth and the life, the one born to live love. This is the characteristic of understanding.

> Then said Jesus, Father, forgive them; for they know not what they do. (St. Luke 23:34)

We can give or forgive only when there is understanding. Jesus with His mind rooted in the Spirit knew and understood that those who called out to crucify Him did not accept Him as the promised Messiah. He knew that when someone is exposed to the truth, they may, or may not, accept or understand. His disciples are a good example.

The disciples were with Him from the beginning. Yet, Judas betrayed Him, and all of them fled when He was arrested, thereby showing their lack of faith even after He had repeatedly told them of their need for faith. However, He knew (understood) that the spirit was willing but the flesh was weak.

More often than not, we find in relationships – be they person to person, male to female, husband to wife, or child to parent – the focus is on right or wrong instead of understanding. I am reminded of a commercial I used to hear. The commercial was created for the purpose of calling drivers' attention to defensive driving. In other words, watch out for the other guy. You as a driver could be in the right. Nevertheless, because of another driver's wrong, you could be killed. Thus, you could be dead. Hence, sometimes we may have to give up the right for the wrong. If you have the green light at an intersection, and the car faced with the red light proceeds without stopping, you would stop, thereby giving way to the wrong. Why? Because, it's better to let the car (which is in the wrong) continue and to avoid an accident than to proceed because you are right and possibly lose your life.

We should take time to consider that "right" could be just as fatal to relationships as "wrong." Many persons have stopped talking or speaking to one another, because they were right and someone did them wrong. Hence, according to God, they do not love. They have

THE DEFINING ELEMENTS OF LOVE

failed in recognizing that God is more concerned with forgiving through understanding than with who is right or wrong.

Finally, be ye all of one mind, having compassion one of another, love as brethren, be pitiful, be courteous: Not rendering evil for evil, or railing for railing: but contrariwise blessing; knowing that ye are thereunto called, that ye should inherit a blessing.

But and if ye suffer for righteousness' sake, happy are ye: and be not afraid of their terror, neither be troubled;

For it is better, if the will of God be so, that ye suffer for well doing, than for evil doing. For Christ also hath once suffered for sins, the just for the unjust, that he might bring us to God, being put to death in the flesh, but quickened by the Spirit: (I Peter 3:8-9, 14, 17-18)

And now this word to all of you: You should be like one happy family, full of sympathy toward each other, loving one another with tender hearts and humble minds. Don't snap back at those who say unkind things about you. Instead, pray for God's help for them, for we are to be kind to others, and God will bless us for it.

Usually no one will hurt you for wanting to do good. But even if they should, you are to be envied, for God will reward you for it.

Remember, if God wants you to suffer, it is better to suffer for doing good than for doing wrong? Christ also suffered. He died once for the sins of all us guilty sinners, although he himself was innocent of any sin at any time, that he might bring us safely home to God. . . . .(1 Peter 3:8-9, 13-14, 17-18 TLB)

The scripture tells us that in all of our getting, we must get understanding. When Jesus said "for they know not what they do," He was saying that He had an understanding but they did not. Therefore, through their misunderstanding of who He was (the promised Messiah), they killed Him.

"THE" DIET FOR YOUR MIND TO HELP YOU FIND THE TRUTH THAT WILL SET YOU FREE

To get an understanding, one must learn to listen. Hence, listening is a key to understanding. The next time you are having a disagreement, instead of defending yourself, or trying to match word for word, just listen. Remember you are seeking an understanding; you are not trying to prove who is right or wrong. I've heard people arguing over the name of a street, only to realize later that it was the same street but the name was changed at a certain point. Because people do not listen, I've heard discussions tantamount to one saying "six" and the opposition saying "half a dozen." These examples may be simple. However, they do happen. They happen because no one is listening and trying to get an understanding.

> Dear brothers, don't ever forget that it is best to listen much, speak little, and not become angry; for anger doesn't make us good, as God demands that we must be. (James 1:19, 20 TLB)

We can also say that understanding is the foundation for giving and forgiving. We give whether we like or dislike a person. We forgive whether the person is right or wrong. Thus, we give and forgive, because we understand that this is what the "will" of the Father would have us do.

Before we can truly comprehend what love is, there must be another recognition. This is not the recognition of an element of love, but rather a positioning of the mind in the spiritual as opposed to the physical when we consider love. This is to say, love has no reason and cannot exist on that which is rooted in the physical. The giving, forgiving and understanding must be born and carried out in and through the spiritual.

When the physical is used as the foundation of love, it has led many to become isolated and cold toward others. A young lady or man sees a physically attractive face or body and allows the superficial – the physical – to persuade them that they love or are in love. Hence, through the physical, by the physical, and of the physical, they build their minds, actions, and beliefs.

Yes, they give, forgive, and understand. However, their action of love and belief of being in love stands on the shaky foundation of the physical. Love that falls into this category (built on the physical) has the endurance of the physical, which is temporal. Thus, when those

THE DEFINING ELEMENTS OF LOVE

who give, forgive and understand because of physical attractiveness learn that the recipient of the same has others who are also giving, forgiving and understanding because of their physical attractiveness, they become hurt, cold and distant. They may vow never to love again. They need only to realize that they never truly loved. Their giving, forgiving, and understanding were for a physical reason. Hence, when reason is considered in love, that love is not love, because, true love has no reason.

In summary, we can say, from examining the life of the one who is the example of love and the pattern to follow in seeking and experiencing love, that to love is to *give, forgive,* and *understand.* We can say that the past centuries were revelations of love in part. Through this writing and through other means, God is trying to help us understand more of the whole.

"THE" DIET FOR YOUR MIND TO HELP YOU FIND THE TRUTH THAT WILL SET YOU FREE

THE ESSENCE OF LOVE

We may have a better understanding of what love is. However, we must seek additional knowledge and wisdom about love if we are to put love into action. Thus, the rationale of giving, forgiving and understanding – the essence of love – must be understood.

When we previously discussed sin we said that sin was **S**-eparation, **I**-solation, and **N**-eutralization. Now we can also say that since sin separates, isolates and neutralizes, it is the opposite of love.

Love will reconcile, reunites and reconnect.

> For the love of Christ constraineth us; because we thus judge, that if one died for all, then were all dead; And that he died for all, that they which live should not henceforth live unto themselves, but unto him which died for them, and rose again. Wherefore henceforth know we no man after the flesh: yea, though we have known Christ after the flesh, yet now henceforth know we him no more. Therefore if any man be in Christ, he is a new creature: old things are passed away; behold, all things are become new. And all things are of God, who hath reconciled us to himself by Jesus Christ, and hath given to us the ministry of reconciliation; To wit, that God was in Christ, reconciling the world unto himself, not imputing their trespasses unto them; and hath committed unto us the word of reconciliation. Now then we are ambassadors for Christ, as though God did beseech you by us: we pray you in Christ's stead, be ye reconciled to God. (II Corinthians 5:14-20)

The essence of love is disharmony finding a way to work in harmony. It is opposites working together: the man and woman, even though different or opposite, having the ability to act and be as one. The essence of love is like the positive pole and the negative pole of a battery working together to store and supply electrical power. It is animals giving off carbon dioxide to plants in order for the plants to live, and the plants giving off oxygen so that animals can live. When

THE ESSENCE OF LOVE

we reflect upon St. John 1:1,14, we can see spiritual opposites (the physical and spiritual) working together; i.e., Jesus or God, the spiritual being, clothed in the flesh (physical) so that together these opposites could accomplish God's work here on earth.

Note that these opposites are able to coexist in harmony because they are able to give to each other. When opposites do their thing without interfering with each other, we have harmony. One of the best examples of different things working in harmony is that of voices singing together. The soprano, alto, tenor, and bass voices can sing together. When they sing together, there is a blending of the voices, which is called harmony. Why and how is this possible? This is possible because, the sopranos have their notes, the altos have their notes, the tenors have their notes, and the same is true with the basses. They each have a different note from the other, but they co-exist. Furthermore, each voice's notes have been chosen with the intention of coexisting and not interfere with one another.

We also can see that each thing or person, even if opposite to ourselves, has a need. The need for the world (the physical) to be saved by Divine (spiritual) guidance in a personality led to the coming of Jesus Christ.

> For the flesh lusteth against the Spirit, and the Spirit against the flesh: and these are contrary the one to the other: so that ye cannot do the things that ye would. (Galatians 5:17)

This scripture says the flesh is against the Spirit. Since the flesh is against (contrary to) the Spirit, does this mean that the flesh and Spirit can't work together? The answer is yes and no. The answer is "no:" the flesh and Spirit cannot work together for good when the flesh – a way of sinful life – is the basis of life, because the mind is not dieting on the spiritual as the way of life. The answer is "yes:" the flesh and Spirit can work together for good when the mind relies upon the sixth sense, thereby doing the things of the Spirit while in the physical body.

So, being opposite or different will not prevent harmony. The man and woman are considered different, but through God they can exist in harmony. We again see that the plant and humanity are different but co-exist. Then we can say that opposites are different and not necessarily contrary.

To be contrary is to be against, opposing, or just simply in conflict. Again, the above scripture says that the flesh and Spirit are contrary to one another. We have also said that when man was created, he was created as flesh (body) and spirit. Then why and when did the parts (flesh and spirit) created to work together as a whole, start to fight against each other?

The conflict arrived when the forbidden fruit was eaten, which caused the world (the physical) and self-consciousness to be activated. The forbidden fruit, the virus to the PCS, allowed the mind to become aware and develop a selfish contrary programming. Thus, man in his original state and fallen state has a body. However, in his original state, man was only aware of God-consciousness, and therefore the mind only had a diet of God's will. Whereas, in the fallen state world-consciousness and self-consciousness were awakened and the mind became subject to the diet of the physical, the world or flesh. This is how those that were created to work in harmony reached the position of being contrary to one another.

The war between the flesh and Spirit is more than a war of harmony against disharmony; it is a war for programming and control of the mind. Will there be a seeking of the Spirit? Will there be a seeking of the way to do unto others as you would have done unto you or of the way to do unto others before they do to you, which is the selfish way (the way of the flesh)?

Hence, we can say that the flesh (the physical) and the Spirit are enemies. Nevertheless, because of the physical's need for divine intervention, the spirit gave to the physical life. In this giving, we can say that God showed love. Furthermore, we can say that God is true to his request of us, "Love (give to) your enemies."

This brings us to one of the biggest problems of life, loving our enemies. The reason most people cannot love their enemies is that they have gotten the types of love mixed up and are confused about love and like. In the book *Strength To Love,* Dr. Martin L. King, Jr., speaks of the types of love.

> The meaning of love is not to be confused with some sentimental outpouring. Love is something much

deeper than emotional bosh. Perhaps the Greek language can clear our confusion at this point. In the Greek New Testament there are three words for love. The word Eros is a sort of aesthetic or romantic love. In the Platonic dialogues eros is a yearning of the soul for the realm of the divine. The second word is philia, a reciprocal love and the intimate affection and friendship between friends. We love those whom we like, and we love because we are loved. The third word is agape, understanding and creative, redemptive goodwill for all men. An overflowing love which seeks nothing in return, agape is the love of God operating in the human heart. At this level, we love men not because their ways appeal to us, nor even because they possess some type of divine spark; we love every man because God loves him. At this level we love the person who does an evil deed, although we hate the deed that he does.[1]

"THE" DIET FOR YOUR MIND TO HELP YOU FIND THE TRUTH THAT WILL SET YOU FREE

LOVE AND LIKE

The above sentence is consistent with the expression, "God hates sin, but loves the sinner." Inasmuch as most people only understand "Eros" love (emotional and physical love), they approach all people through the same. Then to add to their ignorance, they are confused about love and like.

Most of us have grown up with the belief that like is love, only in a lesser degree or measurement. Only when we come to the understanding that love is love and like is like are we able to "love our enemies". God never asked us to "like" anybody. However, He did tell us to love everybody ("your neighbor" – St. Luke 10:30-37). In the previous chapter through and in accordance with the Word of God, we found a workable definition of love. God did not tell us to like everybody. We will turn to Webster's New World Dictionary.

Webster defines like (the verb) as "to be pleased with; enjoy." Like (the adjective) is defined as "similar; having the same characteristics."

When liking is examined closely, we see why like is not a part of loving. When a person says he or she likes someone, it's usually because of something they share in common. Mary likes Jane and Jane likes shopping. Jane likes Mary and Mary likes shopping. Sue likes basketball as well as Carol. Carol likes basketball and attends basketball games with Sue. However, neither Mary nor Sue would be caught dead at a basketball game. Nor would Carol or Sue be caught at malls for hours.

The point here is that the ladies who share a like (for shopping or basketball) find themselves liking each other because of their similar likes. However, loving goes beyond liking or disliking. It involves treating others as you would want to be treated. If Mary or Jane want Carol and Sue to respect them as persons with inalienable rights to be individuals, then it has to be reciprocal. Now Carol and Sue do not like Mary and Jane, but they cannot allow their likes to interfere with love, Agape love.

In *Love, Power, and Justice*[1], Paul Tillich states:

> It is the fulfillment and the triumph of love that is able to reunite the most radically separated beings, namely in individual persons.[2]
>
> In the loving person to person relationship Christianity manifests its superiority to any other religious tradition.[3]
>
> The second principle of justice is that of equality. There is ultimate equality between all men in the view of God and His justice is equally offered to all of them.[4]

Thus love is rooted in the spirit, whereas like is rooted in the physical. We could go further and say that like has reference to the selfish self (the ego). Note that even though you may be born-again, you still have two selves within. Otherwise once we accept Christ (are born-again), we would become perfect. (Please read Romans 7.) Furthermore, to understand I John 5:18 is to recognize that this verse is explaining what Jesus has and is doing. It is not saying that Christians do not sin.

The "selfish *self*" has a right to some things as it is the individuality of life that is given by God. However, the key is to discipline the ego-self so it will not interfere with the God-self. The self has the right to decide who he or she wants to go to the movies with, watch television with, go shopping with, barbeque with, travel with, and so on. In other words, the self has a right to decide who, where, and how it will spend its energy and time. However, love says that even if you do not like a person who asks you for something or has a need, you are to give to the person; if the person does you wrong, you are to forgive the person, and you understand that this is a request from God. Hence, it is not what the self (who fights against God) would do, but what Love ("God is love" I John 4:8) and the God of reuniting would have you do. Once this is understood, then we are able to give to a person, forgive a person, and seek to understand a person, whether or not we desire to spend time and energy on the person or like his or her ways, looks, race, creed, or religion.

I believe that the scriptures we have just reviewed deserve another reading.

> But I say unto you which hear, Love your enemies, do good to them which hate you, (St. Luke 6:27)
>
> Do you think you deserve credit for merely loving those who love you? Even the godless do that! And if you do good only to those who do you good— is that so wonderful? Even sinners do that much! And if you lend money only to those who can repay you, what good is that? Even the most wicked will lend to their own kind for full return! (St. Luke 6:32—34 TLB)
>
> Love your enemies! Do good to them! Lend to them! And don't be concerned about the fact that they won't repay. Then your reward from heaven will be very great, and you will truly be acting as sons of God: for He is kind to the unthankful and to those who are very wicked. (St. Luke 6:35 TLB)

When Jesus taught the disciples about dealing with people they had not chosen to deal with (who were often hated and ridiculed), He did not ask them to like others. He asked them to love others. Remember *liking* means accepting another in the *physical*, whereas *loving* means accepting another in the *spiritual*.

> And upon this came His disciples, and marvelled that He talked with the woman: yet no man said, What seekest thou? or, Why talkest thou with her? (St. John 4:27)

When I first read the above verse, my soul was troubled as to why the disciples marvelled at Jesus' talking to the woman. Did they overhear Jesus trying to hit on the woman? Did they feel that something was transpiring between the woman and Jesus that was contrary to Jesus' teaching? After prayer and meditation, the Holy Spirit revealed the truth of the occurrence. The key is found in verse nine (9) of the chapter.

> Then saith the woman of Samaria unto Him, How is it that thou, being a Jew, askest drink of me, which am a woman of Samaria? for the Jews have no dealings with the Samaritans. (St. John 4:9)

Jesus' talking with the woman was not contrary to His teaching, nor was He relating to her in the physical. The marveling by the

LOVE AND LIKE

disciples was because the woman was a Samaritan. Jesus and the disciples were Jews. The above verse says that the Jews had nothing to do with the Samaritans. Jesus was a Jew and talking to a Samaritan was shocking to the disciples. Nevertheless, through this and other similar actions, Jesus taught the disciples – you and me today – not to let undisciplined like interfere with love.

Again we must remind ourselves that even though we have accepted Jesus as Lord and Savior, because we are born-again, there can still be dislike of others because of their race, creed or religion. We can look and find Peter, one of Jesus' disciples, who walked and talked as well as received direct teachings from Jesus, but yet continued with prejudice – dislike – for fellow human beings who were not Jews like himself. This dislike is what causes the person being disliked to be identified as an enemy.

In Caesarea there lived a Roman army officer, Cornelius, a captain of an Italian regiment. He was a godly man, deeply reverent, as was his entire household. He gave generously to charity and was a man of prayer. While wide awake one afternoon he had a vision – it was about three o'clock – and in this vision he saw an angel of God coming toward him. "Cornelius!" the angel said. Cornelius stared at him in terror. "What do you want, sir?" he asked the angel. And the angel replied, "Your prayers and charities have not gone unnoticed by God! Now send some men to Joppa to find a man named Simon Peter, who is staying with Simon, the tanner, down by the shore, and ask him to come and visit you."

As soon as the angel was gone, Cornelius called two of his household servants and a godly soldier, one of his personal bodyguard, and told them what had happened and sent them off to Joppa. The next day, as they were nearing the city, Peter went up on the flat roof of the house to pray. It was noon and he was hungry, but while lunch was being prepared, he fell into a trance. He saw the sky open, and a great canvas sheet, suspended by its four corners, settle to the ground. In the sheet were all sorts of animals, snakes and birds [forbidden to the Jews for food]. Then a voice said to him, "Go kill and eat any of them you wish." "Never. Lord," Peter declared, "I have never in all my life eaten such creatures, for they are forbidden by our Jewish laws." The voice spoke again, "Don't contradict God! If he says something is kosher, then it is." The same vision was repeated three times. Then the sheet was pulled up again to heaven. Peter was very perplexed. What could the vision mean? What was he supposed to do? Just then the men sent by Cornelius had found the house and were standing outside at the gate, inquiring whether this was the place where Simon Peter lived! Meanwhile, as Peter was puzzling over the vision, the Holy Spirit said to him, "Three men have come to see you. Go down and meet them and go with them. All is well, I have sent them." So Peter went down. "I'm the man you're looking for," he said. "Now what is it you want?" They told him about Cornelius the Roman officer, a good and godly man, well thought of by the Jews, and how an angel had instructed him to send for Peter to come and tell him to send for Peter to come and tell what God wanted him to do. So Peter invited them in and lodged them overnight. The next day he went with them, accompanied by some other believers from Joppa. They arrived in Caesarea the following day, and Cornelius was waiting for him, and had called together his relatives and close friends to meet Peter. As Peter entered his home, Cornelius fell to the floor before him in worship. But Peter said, "Stand up! I'm not a god!" So he got up and they talked together for a while and then went in where the others were assembled. Peter told them, "You know it is against the Jewish laws for me to come into a Gentile home like this. But God has shown me in a vision that I should never think of

LOVE AND LIKE

anyone as inferior. So I came as soon as I was sent for. Now tell me what you want."

Cornelius replied, "Four days ago I was praying as usual at this time of the afternoon, when suddenly a man was standing before me clothed in a radiant robe! He told me, 'Cornelius, your prayers are heard and your charities have been noticed by God! Now send some men to Joppa and summon Simon Peter, who is staying in the home of Simon, a tanner, down by the shore.' So I sent for you at once, and you have done well to come so soon. Now here we are, waiting before the Lord, anxious to hear what he has told you to tell us!" Then Peter replied, "I see very clearly that the Jews are not God's only favorites! In every nation he has those who worship him and do good deeds and are acceptable to him. I'm sure you have heard about the good news for the people of Israel that there is peace with God through Jesus, the Messiah, who is Lord of all creation. The message has spread all through Judea, beginning with John the Baptist in Galilee.

And he sent us to preach the good news everywhere and to testify that Jesus is ordained of God to be the Judge of all –living and dead. And all the prophets have written about him, saying that everyone who believes in him will have their sins forgiven through his name. Even as Peter was saying these things, the Holy Spirit fell upon all those listening! The Jews who came with Peter were amazed that the gift of the Holy Spirit would be given to Gentiles too! But there could be no doubt about it, for they heard them speaking in tongues and praising God. (Acts 10:1-37,42-47 TLB)

Furthermore, Peter had observed a similar teaching when the Syrophenician woman approached Jesus.

Then he left and went to the region of Tyre and Sidon, and tried to keep it a secret that he was there, but couldn't. For as usual the news of his arrival spread

"THE" DIET FOR YOUR MIND TO HELP YOU FIND THE TRUTH THAT WILL SET YOU FREE

fast. Right away a woman came to him whose little girl was possessed by a demon. She had heard about Jesus and now she came and fell at his feet, and pled with him to release her child from the demon's control. (But she was Syrophoenician – a "despised Gentle!") Jesus told her, "First I should help my own family – the Jews. It isn't right to take the children's food and throw it to the dogs." She replied, "That's true, sir, but even the puppies under the table are given some scraps from the children's plates." "Good!" he said, "You have answered well – so well that I have healed your little girl. Go on home, for the demon has left her!" And when she arrived home, her little girl was lying quietly in bed, and the demon was gone. (St. Mark 7:24-30 TLB)

The preceding scriptures are used to show two things. The first is that, even though Peter was with Jesus when Jesus was speaking with the Samarian woman, as mentioned above, and had witnessed Jesus' giving to the despised, through the Syrophoenician woman, he continued in his belief of prejudice toward other races (Gentiles). The second thing the scriptures show is that Peter's acceptance of a different race came through the Spirit of God.

In *Strength to Love*[5], Dr. King states why we should love our enemies. He says, "Hate for hate multiplies hate, adding deeper darkness to night already devoid of stars." "The chain reaction of evil – hate begetting hate, wars producing more wars – must be broken, or we shall be plunged into the dark abyss of annihilation." Thus, Dr. King is saying hate plus hate equals "HATE." Therefore, only when hate is faced with love, inasmuch as love is more powerful than hate (love conquers all), can we avoid annihilation and have opposites coexisting.

Dr. King's second reason why we should love our enemies is that, "Hate scars the souls and distorts the personality." Furthermore, hate not only does irreparable damage to its victims but, "Hate is just as injurious to the person who hates." Hence there is distortion of values and confusion when faced with truth and falsehoods. In other words, when a person refuses to give, forgive, and understand another, he or she is not recognizing that we are all humans, but is thinking of himself or herself as better than the other person. Consequently, the false idea of "better" causes confusion with the truth that we all are "equal" in God's eyesight, according to the Manual.

> There is neither Jew nor Greek, there is neither bond nor free, there is neither male nor female: for ye are all one in Christ Jesus. *(Galatians 3:28)*

Dr. King goes on to say, "A third reason why we should love our enemies is that love is the only force capable of transforming an enemy into a friend." Again, if we meet hate with hate we end with hate. If we love (give to) only those who love (give to) us, the adversary is still an adversary. However, when we employ the force of love (put love into action), the adversary becomes a friend.

Dr. King, like myself and everyone else who has found an insight into love, had to turn to the spiritual to truly explain why we should love our enemies.

> We must hasten to say that these are not the ultimate reasons why we should love our enemies. An even more basic reason why we are commanded to love is expressed explicitly in Jesus' words, "Love your enemies …that ye may be children of your Father which is in Heaven." We are called to this difficult task in order to realize a unique relationship with God. Through love that potentially becomes actuality. We must love our enemies, because only by loving them can we know God and experience the beauty of His holiness.[6]

Even in personal relationships, opposites must seek harmony. We have already said the '60s' "free love" and the '70s' "do your own thing" were failures. Furthermore, all giving and all receiving were failures. The failures of these were a direct result of the lack of balance and harmony. The free love attitude brought the erroneous thought that giving and not receiving is all. Thus, the needs of each person involved were not being identified or satisfied. The parties were so busy giving that neither was receiving and consequently, both became miserable.

"THE" DIET FOR YOUR MIND TO HELP YOU FIND THE TRUTH THAT WILL SET YOU FREE

    The principle – give without expecting anything in return – is the foundation of love. However, the giving experienced during the '60s was purely physical and without spiritual understanding.

    Then the '70's – the time of "do your own thing" – arrived and an about face was taken. The "do your own thing" was the exact opposite of "free love." Free love was based upon reaching out to others in the physical, by the physical, and for the physical. It was denying the self the opportunity to receive but not through the spiritual. The '70s said, "I have denied the self and I am empty. Now I will seek satisfaction of the self regardless of the other's needs." The result was the return of true selfishness – the seeking of what is to one's own advantage only.

    Emptiness was the bottom line of the '70s as it was in the '60s. When the self reached out to satisfy itself, it met with similar selves doing the same. "You do your thing and I'll do mine" was the motto. Maybe in the twenty-first century, we will find the acceptable year of the Lord. In that year, we will truly come to know what love is. This will be the year we learn to give. In that year, we'll find something in another's gender, male or female, in another's race, white or black, in another's religion, Catholic or Protestant, which we can use to meet a need. This will be the year we can say, I love (I'll give, forgive, and understand) you, even though I don't like you. I can do this because I've learned "Agape" (spiritual) Love.

FIRST CORINTHIANS THIRTEEN

We could never attempt to understand love without going into the thirteenth chapter of First Corinthians. Therein, the Apostle Paul gives the church at Corinth an explanation of what love is and is not. He enunciates the behavior or characteristics of love. Thus, when we dissect this chapter, we are able to see things that are done which can be said not to be love, and things that are done which exemplify love.

Love Does:

Suffereth Long	—has patience
Is Kind	—has sympathy – ability to share another's ideas and emotions
Rejoiceth In Truth	—never lies
Believeth All Things	—supports the other person, is loyal to the other person
Hopeth All Things	—walks by faith with the person, not by sight
Endureth All Things	—continues with another during good times and bad times
Never Faileth	—never abandons the person, even if it means giving of life.

Love Does Not:

Envy	—desires what belongs to another for the self
Vaunt	—boasts of the self or is proud of the self
Puff Up	—praises the self
Behave Unseemly	—acts indecently or unbecomingly
Seek Its Own	—is not selfish
Easily Provoked	—is easily made angry or irritated
Think Evil	—has thoughts that are harmful
Rejoice In Iniquity	—is happy about evil or wickedness

"THE" DIET FOR YOUR MIND TO HELP YOU FIND THE TRUTH THAT WILL SET YOU FREE

In the examination, note that when you examine each thing love does, the basic elements of love – giving and forgiving, through understanding – can be found. To illustrate this point let us take the first that is mentioned: suffereth long (has patience).

The dictionary gives a definition of suffering as undergoing, experiencing, putting up with, especially as inevitable or unavoidable; allowing, especially by reason of indifference.

Thus, to put up with indifferences and undergo the experience of trying to get along with another human who is capable of existing on his or her own, the opposite of trying to become one, a person has to be able to give, forgive and understand. The giving may just be giving of time, or energy, or some word that eventually finds the recipient changing his or her attitude or perspective on life.

The forgiving is found when another does a wrong to the giver – when behavior by another lacks the elements of love. Understanding is found when the giver recognizes that because there were no models, or because of a failure on the part of the receiver to appreciate what the giver was trying to accomplish in the relationship, the receiver did not know what the giver did. Hence, there is suffering that accompanies the giving; but forgiving through understanding allows patience.

Examining this chapter and bringing out the "what is" and the "what is not" love, without understanding the eleventh (11th) verse would be to suffer a great loss. For it is in this verse that the true contrast of "love" and "not love" is stated.

> When I was a child, I spake as a child, I understood as a child, I thought as a child: but when I became a man, I put away childish things. (I Corinthians 13:11)

Here lies the one stumbling block for those who never find love, and the hurdle that had to be overcome by those who did find love. If we are to truly understand the truth of this verse, we must examine a child's behavior and contrast that behavior with the proper adult behavior.

When we examine a child's behavior we find that his or her life consist of selfishness. Please note that, here, we are not being critical of the behavior, but rather seeking the truth. This writer realizes that this behavior is the normal behavior of a child.

Being selfish is defined in the dictionary as being overly concerned with one's own interest and advantages, so that the welfare of others is neglected.

A child is only concerned with being comforted, with getting a bottle, having his diaper changed and sleeping; a child is concerned with receiving for the self regardless of the inconveniences caused to another. He will get the attention of those around him to have these things done by crying, screaming or throwing things. Once the child has grown beyond the necessities, he or she does not stop there. Next, is the "throwing a tantrum" or "throwing a fit" stage. The tantrum stage carries with it a behavior similar to a new born. However, now the behavior is not initiated out of necessity, but rather, out of wanting to have his or her own interests and desires satisfied.

When the child was an infant if he wanted a bottle, he cried and the bottle was delivered shortly thereafter. Now he is beyond infancy but seeks to accomplish receiving through an infants' behavior. He wants a piece of candy, and for whatever reason, the parents refuse to give it to him. Thus, the child cries, screams, falls down, rolls on the floor and so on to get what he desires. As mentioned before and as stated in the above eleventh verse, this is all right when we are children. However, according to the scripture, one should give up this behavior when one grows beyond the childhood years. When one grows to adulthood one should realize the truth in the scripture that "it is better to give than to receive." (Acts 20:35) One must find equal, or more enjoyment in giving. As a child, one wants just for the self, just to receive. As an adult one should realize that in truth, in the higher planes of life, in spirituality where man was originally created to roam within, the proper thing to do is give.

In Genesis, God created the earth and all therein and gave man dominion over the same. Furthermore, after man caused separation between himself and God, God gave his only begotten Son to reconcile man back to Himself. There was suffering by God in the giving. However, God cares for all of His creation. Therefore, He knew when He created man that man would cause Him suffering. Nevertheless, He gave man life and man gave himself death. Then through the giving of His Son He gave man a second chance to have eternal life.

"THE" DIET FOR YOUR MIND TO HELP YOU FIND THE TRUTH THAT WILL SET YOU FREE

God has patience with us. This patience is grounded in love. He's patient in allowing us to accept His Son as Lord and Savior. Then His patience is shown when after accepting Christ, some turn back and all of us fall short of His glory. However, regardless of our behavior whether in conformity or disobedience to His Word, He never stops giving, forgiving or understanding, giving us all our needs in life, forgiving us all our sins in life and understanding that the spirit is willing, but so often the flesh is weak. Indeed, the Father, Son and Holy Spirit have shown us the way, the truth, the life, and the true meaning of love.

We are to find joy in giving as well as receiving. We are to learn that to want only for the self is to make oneself dull and intolerable. Thus, to give is to love and this is learned when one looks around at one's surroundings and sees what has been given for one's enjoyment and comfort: the air we breathe, the sun that lights and warms our day, even life itself. Then, we should desire to be in life like the Heavenly Father – giving, even when it meant the giving of His only begotten Son.

The act of giving must be done freely without coercion or expectation of receiving anything in return. However, in St. Luke, you'll find that when there is a return of His favor to you, it will be compounded; what you receive (blessings) will be as much as you gave and indeed much more.

> Try to show as much compassion as your Father does. Never criticize or condemn – or it will all come back to you. Go easy on others; then they will do the same for you. For if you give, you will get! Your gift will return to you in full and overflowing measure, pressed down, shaken together to make room for more, and running over. Whatever measure you use to give – large or small – will be used to measure what is given back to you. (St. Luke 6:36-38 TLB)

This scripture is used to point out the fringe benefits of love – to point out the positive nature of love before love is perceived as a negative. However, the scripture is intentionally reserved about the direct benefits of love in order to have the mind seek love for love and not for its benefits. Thus, if you love and you have reached this page without knowing the benefits of love, God has already begun to shine through. But, if you have at least reached this page in hope of eventually finding the fringe benefits of love, then thank God for the revelation.

Thomas, who was one of Jesus' disciples, also doubted. He said he would only believe that Jesus had risen from the dead if he could place his finger in the nail prints of Jesus' hand and side where He was pierced. Jesus gave Thomas that experience and said:

> "You believe because you have seen me. But blessed are those who haven't seen me and believe anyway." (St. John 20:29 TLB)

The above says we are blessed because we see and therefore believe, and even more so when we believe before seeing.

Often as a minister I am asked, "Why don't church people get along better with one another?" The answer that the Spirit revealed to me was, "They don't love." People are more interested in getting back at each other than getting an understanding. They are too interested in what they can receive, instead of what they can give. Thus, this selfish attitude leads them to the desire to be forgiven for their wrongs, but they find it beneath their pride to forgive the wrong done to them by others.

> Then came Peter to him, and said, Lord, how oft shall my brother sin against me, and I forgive him? till seven times? Jesus saith unto him, I say not unto thee, Until seven times: but, Until seventy times seven. (St. Matthew 18:21—22)

> Bretheren, if a man be overtaken in a fault, ye which are spiritual, restore such as one in the spirit of meekness; considering thyself, lest thou also be tempted. Bear ye one another's burdens, and so fulfill the law of Christ. (Galatians 6:1—2)

To seek love is not hard at all. But to live love means getting rid of self (the ego) and this is where the battle takes place. Let's revisit Romans.

> I don't understand myself at all, for I really want to do what is right, but I can't. I do what I don't want to—what I hate. I know perfectly well that what I am doing is

wrong, and my bad conscience proves that I agree with these laws I am breaking. But I can't help myself, because I'm no longer doing it. It is sin inside me that is stronger than I am that makes me do these evil things.

I know I am rotten through and through so far as my old sinful nature is concerned. No matter which way I turn I can't make myself do right. I want to but I can't. When I want to do good, I don't; and when I try not to do wrong, I do it anyway. Now if I am doing what I don't want to, it is plain where the trouble is: sin still has me in its evil grasp.

It seems to be a fact of life that when I want to do what is right, I inevitably do what is wrong. I love to do God's will so far as my new nature is concerned; but there is something else deep within me, in my lower nature, that is at war with my mind and wins the fight and makes me a slave to the sin that is still within me. In my mind I want to be God's willing servant but instead I find myself still enslaved to sin.

So you see how it is: my new life tells me to do right, but the old nature that is still inside me loves to sin. Oh, what a terrible predicament I'm in! Who will free me from my slavery to this deadly lower nature? Thank God! It has been done by Jesus Christ our Lord. He has set me free.

Through Paul, God taught us that this fight has to be fought and won by Jesus. Again, this is why love must be sought, learned and acted upon and must be rooted in the spirit. This is because the flesh is disobedient to God. This is the purpose of being born again. The old self-flesh – which we are born of in the first birth, could not, would not, and never has listened and obeyed God. So a birth by, through, and of, the spirit is needed. Thus, we then have a chance to let Jesus – who is love – live inside of us.

Therefore, if any man be in Christ, he is a new creature: old things are passed away; behold, all things are become new. (II Corinthians 5:17)

> I am crucified with Christ: nevertheless I live; yet not I, but Christ liveth in me: the life which I now live in the flesh I live by the faith of the Son of God, who loved me, and gave himself for me. (Galatians 2:20)

Once we have learned to "let go" and "let God" the battle becomes the Lord's. Hence, if you want love according to the Spirit, you desire to receive love by the Spirit, all you have to do is ask the heavenly Father in Jesus' name and it will be granted. This must be done in faith.

One other thing must be pointed out before you begin this seeking. When you ask God to help you learn anything that will help you grow in Christ, the Lord will allow certain things to happen in your life. To increase your faith, maybe God will allow your money to depreciate to a point that you will have to rely on God instead of your bank account. The same could happen with love. If you are married, God may allow you to see all the selfishness in your spouse, which may be a reflection on yourself. Remember all concepts, learning and everything start with self. Therefore, you may be seeing the selfishness in him or her, but God is saying the same exists in you.

In *Secret of Secrets*, U.S. Andersen[1] lays down a truth that opened my heart and mind to learning about myself. Anderson says all action is for a purpose. Everything is moving according to God's will and God's control. Hence, when we see something in the world that needs changing, in truth it is not the world but the one who sees it that needs changing. When we see something in someone else that we perceive as in need of change, then it is a reflection of what needs to be changes in ourselves. The world – other people – is only acting many times as a mirror, a reflection of what exists within the holder (you) of the mirror.

Then there is the possibility of God working with both of you simultaneously. Therefore, when you find yourself and a mate, spouse or friend arguing about the other's behavior, stop and think a moment. Give each other a chance to give the evidence of the accusation. If the evidence is true, then listen and learn. Because, if you don't learn from this argument, there will be plenty more. How do I know? I know because, I have learned that a person must learn from lessons in life if there is to be growth in his or her life. The person's name might

"THE" DIET FOR YOUR MIND TO HELP YOU FIND THE TRUTH THAT WILL SET YOU FREE

change, but the situation will not change. In our quest to grow in Christ, we must take one step, one lesson, and one day at a time. We will not be allowed to know the deeper spiritual things of life until we learn of the lesser spiritual things. As man's school will not allow entrance into the tenth grade until completion of the ninth grade, so it is in God's school, life. So, seek not in one another who is right or wrong, but seek growth in Christ. And remember God teaches us through experiences.

One night while teaching a bible class, I had the class turn to Galatians 5:22-23 and pointed out to them one of the most overlooked fruit of the spirit by most Christians: the one fruit that is shunned. The fruit that no one wants to confess. Nevertheless, it is had with all the other fruit. The fruit is longsuffering.

Unless a person possesses masochistic tendencies, he/she does not like pain. Yet pain is as much a part of life as birth and death. But pain will not last always. The reference here is made to admonish you that pain and pleasure are like love and marriage. They go together. One paradox that often plagued me was:

> For whosoever will save his life shall lose it; but whosoever shall lose his life for my sake and the gospel's, the same shall save it. (St. Mark 8:35)

How could you lose you life and yet gain your life? And then there is another paradox that says, "To reach the greatest heights you have to reach the greatest depths." I thank God, the Holy Spirit for helping me understand these two paradoxes. The latter only means that you must undergo certain tests (allowed by God) if you are to understand things of God. The former simply means that to have life and more abundantly life – eternal life – we have to die (get rid of the self). Let God's will be our will and follow the way, the truth, and the life – Jesus Christ. Again, it is not I who live, but Christ who lives inside me.

Sometimes, we must experience rain to appreciate the sun. Sometimes, we must experience not having to appreciate having, and we must experience pain to appreciate pleasure. Most times in our striving for love, joy, peace, gentleness, goodness, faith, meekness, and temperance (the fruit of the spirit) we must experience, or obtain them through long suffering (the other fruit of the Spirit). So what is experiencing a little pain from extraction of a tooth, when the extraction was necessary for the health of the person? After the tooth is removed, the person is able to eat foods that may previously not have been edible. The long suffering of love is also beneficial. Thus a paradox is appropriate here, "The end justifies the means." So, if you suffer in your attempt to find love, remember, the sun will come out tomorrow, and be thankful that in your expression of love, your long suffering does not have to consist of having to wear a thorny crown, being nailed to a cross and pierced in the side. Yet, this was the long suffering of my Lord and Savior, Jesus Christ. The scripture says He even sweated drops of blood. (St Luke 22:44) Furthermore, consider how long Jesus waits for a person to accept him as Lord and savior. Then, after He is accepted, consider how long He endures our lack of spiritual knowledge and growth in Christ.

His giving, even when it was His all (His life), without any childish behavior, is the example of love we are to follow. We, as followers of His leadership, should put away selfishness and walk in the spirit of mature love. As we look to Jesus, we realize His suffering was accepted without any behavior that could be characterized as childish. We, as followers of His leadership, should do the same. We should put away childishness and selfishness and walk in the Spirit seeking "what love does" while denying "what love does not." Thus, looking to First Corinthians Thirteen as one of our references in the practice of love.

"THE" DIET FOR YOUR MIND TO HELP YOU FIND THE TRUTH THAT WILL SET YOU FREE

WHAT'S LOVE GOT TO DO WITH IT?

During the '60s a song was written and released to the world, *What The World Needs Now is Love, Sweet Love.*[1] As a representative of God and believing the truth found in the Holy Bible – God is love – I must concur with the words of the song.

When the cry went out for love in the '60s, the world responded with "free love." There was an attempt to reach out and love one another. However, as previously mentioned, the attempt was rooted in the wrong source. Nevertheless, this free love started a new era of the world's approach to love. We could say this was the birth or beginning of the world (the masses) eagerly and earnestly seeking love. Thus, this new approach or attempt of the world to understand love had begun as a newborn child.

As previously mentioned, the child made an about face in the '70s. Instead of love growing in the perspective of giving, it turned into a selfish spoiled brat and sought only its own self-interest. Thus, instead of growing in the proper direction, it began a regression, a backsliding, making situations worse. Hence, the '60s were rooted in how much one could give, according to the physical, and the '70s were rooted in how much one could receive according to the physical.

Then, in the middle of the '80s this child (love) – new life – had been around about twenty years. It may have been twenty years old, but it had not grown. The rationale supporting this position is found in the success of a song released in the middle of the '80s, *What's Love Got To Do With It?* This song in 1984 was voted song of the year by the physical world. However, from a spiritual perspective, I see the popularity of this song asking us spiritually, *What's Love Got To Do With It.* Furthermore, this song of the year not only asked the question of the year but also probably asked the question of the decade, the century, the existence of life. Giving and understanding on the surface – the physical – have led to frustration. But, before you abandon the greatest of all gifts (love), let us try giving and forgiving according to holy understanding.

Life for the most part is trial and error. Thus the saying, "To err is human and to forgive is divine," is useful in our walk through life. We

WHAT'S LOVE GOT TO DO WITH IT?

make mistakes but are not destroyed. So, we say the "free love" was a bummer. "Doing my own thing" was frustrating. Maybe after truly understanding what love is, we can also understand what love's got to do with it; then the frustration would not have been in vain.

When the world sent out a cry, the cry seemed to be rooted in pain. The question "What's love got to do with it?" appeared to be crying out for an answer. However, we, the representatives of God, did not respond. This lack of response disturbs me, because if we were to analyze the words cried out from the world, we would find within the question destitution, loneliness, bitterness and anger. There are times when Christians must listen to the world's cry and lend assistance; after all, we are the salt of the earth.

The source of the cry is not significant. Who knows why the cry came in the form of music. Who knows why it came from an African-American singer. Who knows why it came out near a time assassins had attempted to kill the President of the United States and the Pope, the head of the largest Christian following in the world. Why did such a question come out? The question we know came from the physical world, but the answer may have to come from a deeper source, the spiritual world.

The late Marvin Gaye asked the question "What's Going On?"[2] and a few years later found his answer in "Sexual Healing."[3] The voice of God, through one of His servants, spoke out and said the answer was "spiritual healing." Yet, when the voice cries out, "What's love got to do with it," the voice of God has not been heard. Has the church forgotten that God is love? Could it be that those of us who represent God are also wondering, "What's going on?" Inasmuch as the answer has not been found, our seeking has brought us to ask the question, "What's love got to with it?" However, if we were to rid ourselves of self-consciousness and world-consciousness and program our PCS to God-consciousness, our answer can only be, love has "everything" to do with it.

> For God so loved the world, that He gave His only begotten Son, that whosoever believeth in Him should not perish, but have everlasting life. For God sent His Son not into the world to condemn the world; but that

"THE" DIET FOR YOUR MIND TO HELP YOU FIND THE TRUTH THAT WILL SET YOU FREE

the world through Him might be saved. (St. John 3:16-17)

This writing has already given an explanation why God as Jesus came into this physical world for those who may not be believers in Jesus Christ. Hence, when you respond to the above scripture with "so what?" remember your objective is to go into the spiritual to understand what through the physical we have misused and misunderstood. However, again we will examine the alpha to understand the reason Jesus was given as a sacrifice for the world and its relevance to love as we approached an understanding through a holy understanding of the alpha.

> In the beginning God created the heaven and the earth. So God created man in his own image, in the image of God created he him; male and female created he them. (Genesis 1:1,27)

If you were to read the entire first and second chapter of Genesis, or review some of the previous chapters herein, you would find that God created everything: the lights, heavens, earth, seas, grass, trees, sun, moon, stars, creatures of the waters, fowl of the air, creatures of the earth, as well as man and woman. Inasmuch as we have learned that God is love, when we hear the question "What's love got to with it?" we are actually asking, "What's God got to do with it?" The above scripture stated that God created all. Hence, God has everything to do with all.

After God had finished His creating, and everything God created was perfect, He gave man dominion over all and a commandment.

> And the Lord God commanded the man, saying, Of every tree of the garden thou mayest freely eat: But of the tree of the knowledge of good and evil, thou shall not eat of it: for in the day thou eatest thereof thou shalt surely die. (Genesis 2:16-17)

The woman (Eve) deceived by the serpent, and man (Adam) whom God created, ate of the forbidden fruit. Thus, they were disobedient and fell from God's grace. Thereby, they became sinful creatures because of the awakening of conscience.

> And the serpent said unto the woman, Ye shall not surely die, For God doth know that the day ye eat

thereof, then your eyes shall be opened, and ye shall be as gods, knowing good and evil. And when the woman saw that the tree was good for food, and that it was pleasant to the eyes, and a tree to be desired to make one wise, she took of the fruit thereof, and did eat, and gave also unto her husband with her; and he did eat. (Genesis 3:4—6)

The sin of disobedience began the virus in the PCS (worldly consciousness and self-consciousness) that would lead to many other sins. Furthermore, sin, itself, caused three lasting side effects. The side effects were: 1) man was separated from God; 2) man had to make a sacrifice to God for sin; and 3) death was given temporary victory.

1) Man's Separation from God

Behold, the Lord's hand is not shortened, that it cannot save; neither is his ear heavy, that it cannot hear: But your iniquities have separated between you and your God, and your sins have hid his face from you, that he will not hear. (Isaiah 59:1-2)

The scripture reveals that sin comes between God and man, thereby, causing the fellowship between man and God to be broken (separation). If you have ever visited cities such as Philadelphia, San Francisco and others, you may understand this separation through the principles involved with the cable cars. To make the example simple, let's say God is the power line from which the cable cars receive their power to move and the cable cars are the persons. Whenever the cable cars lose contact with the power line there is no movement, no life, no receiving. Thus sin is the disconnector and comes between (interferes) with the car (person) and the power (God).

Hence, when Adam and Eve sinned, they caused evil to come between God and man. We must make note that man caused the separation between God and himself. However, it was God who provided the means for restoring fellowship. Furthermore, it was not an army, nor physical weapon, nor any other type of coercion that

God used as the instrument to bring mankind back to Himself. Rather, it was the most powerful force that exists. It was love.

2) Sacrifice to God for Sin

The need for God to restore the broken fellowship led to the requirement of atonement. In the Old Testament (covenant), atonement was achieved through animal sacrifice. There is no remission of sin without the shedding of blood.

> And almost all things are by the law purged with blood; and without shedding of blood there is no remission. (Hebrews 9:22)
>
> And thou shalt offer every day a bullock for a sin offering for atonement; and thou shalt cleanse the altar, when thou hast made an atonement for it, and thou shall anoint it, to sanctify it. (Exodus 29:36)
>
> And the priest shall make an atonement for him before the Lord: and it shall be forgiven him for anything of all that he hath done in trespassing therein. (Leviticus 6:7)

The Old Testament was only a shadow or symbolic of what was to come. The bullock, birds, goats, and lambs according to the sin, were used as the sacrifice. As stated above in the scriptures, the sacrifice was made for atonement or forgiveness of sin. The New Covenant or agreement fulfilled the old by one sacrifice. This sacrifice was the Son of God, Jesus Christ.

> For the law having a shadow of good things to come, and not the very image of the things, can never with those sacrifices which they offered year by year continually make the comer thereunto perfect. For it is not possible that the blood of bulls and of goats should take away sins. Wherefore when he cometh into the world he saith, Sacrifice and offering thou wouldest not, but a body hast thou prepared me: In burnt-offerings and sacrifices for sin thou hast had no pleasure. Then said I, Lo, I come (in volume of the book it is written of me,) to do thy will, O God.

WHAT'S LOVE GOT TO DO WITH IT?

> Then said he, Lo, I come to do thy will, O God. He taketh away the first, that he may establish the second. By the which will we are sanctified through the offering of the body of Jesus Christ once and for all. (Hebrews 10:1, 4-7, 9-10)

If we read Ephesians 1:4-7, we will find that He was the lamb of sacrifice for love. Furthermore, through His blood there is the possibility that we can be re-united with God as His children. The Godly and human family can exist again.

> According as he hath chosen us in him before the foundation of the world, that we should be holy and without blame before him in love: Having predestined us unto adoption of children by Jesus Christ to himself, according to the good pleasure of his will, To the praise of the glory of his grace, wherein he hath made us accepted in the beloved. In whom we have redemption through his blood, the forgiveness of sins according to the riches of his grace; (Ephesians 1:4-7)

The sacrifice, Jesus, was given for the forgiveness of sin through God understanding the need. As stated above, this was and is done through what is called love.

3) Death and Victory

The third lasting effect upon mankind, the result of sin, was and is death. The "and is" is in effect if one has not accepted Jesus as sacrifice for one's sin.

> For the wages of sin is death; but the gift of God is eternal life through Jesus Christ our Lord. (Romans 6:23)

If we were to refer to Genesis 2:17, we would find that God told Adam this would be the consequence of his disobedience. Thank God for His Son, Jesus Christ. Christ was obedient, and lived a perfect life, thereby, becoming the perfect lamb for sacrifice.

> For as by one man's disobedience many were made sinners, so by the obedience of one shall many be made righteous. (Romans 5:19)

> Who, being in the form of God, thought it not robbery to be equal with God. But made himself of no reputation, and took upon him the form of a servant, and was made in the likeness of men: And being found in fashion as a man, he humbled himself, and became obedient unto death, even the death of the cross. (Philippians 2:6-8)

Yes, death had become man's greatest enemy. Man and woman sinned. Thus, death has the sting and the grave, the victory. There has to be a way back to the tree of life. Only love could remove the flaming sword that turned in every direction to keep man from the tree of life; as stated in *Genesis 3:22—24 above.*

Jesus' life, death and resurrection, were the combination necessary for mankind to obtain the right or access to the tree of life, or everlasting life.

> So when this corruptible shall have put on incorruption, and this mortal shall have put on immortality, then shall be brought to pass the saying that is written, Death is swallowed up in victory. O death, where is thy sting? O grave, where is thy victory? The sting of death is sin; and the strength of sin is the law. But thanks be to God, which giveth us the victory through our Lord Jesus Christ. (I Corinthians 15:54-57)

Our hope and possibility of life after death is found in the purpose for which Christ was manifested. Through Christ, and only through Christ, can we be born of the Spirit.

> Jesus answered, Verily, verily, I say unto thee, Except a man be born of water and of the Spirit, he cannot enter into the kingdom of God. That which is born of the flesh is flesh; and that which is born of the Spirit is spirit. The wind bloweth where it listeth, and thou hearest the sound thereof, but canst not tell whence it cometh, whither it goeth: so is everyone that is born of the Spirit. (St. John 3:5—6, 8)

"In the beginning was the Word, and the Word was with God, and the Word was God. And the Word was made flesh, and dwelt among us, full of grace and truth." (St. John 1:1, 14) Jesus had to come from heaven, conquer death, and return to the heavenly Father. Indeed, God so loved the world that He gave His only begotten Son to save the world.

One of the main ingredients we have recognized in love is giving. This giving goes beyond one's time, energy, and self. The giving is often found in the giving of a gift. God has shown us and taught us to give. His gift was His only begotten Son. Therefore, to fully understand love, we have to accept this gift. Once one has accepted the gift and become familiar with the gift, one understands what love has got to do with it.

Finally, when we realize that God created all, we understand that to ask what love (God) has got to do with it is to ask what's GMC got to do with Cadillac, or what's Ford got to do with Thunderbird, or what's Burger King got to do with the Whopper, or what's McDonalds got to do with the Big Mac. The creator made the thing and knows what's best for the creation.

Hence, God created all, even when all was lost. All have sinned and fallen short of God's glory, and He gave His all to save all. So, we may say love (God) has everything to do with it.

Another reason, I believe, many ask this question about love is the misunderstanding and misapplication of a simple principle: you reap what you sow.

I was born, and spent my early childhood days, in the rural part of Georgia. There, my father taught me one principle of nature. The principle was, what you planted would be what you harvested (received). Corn seeds planted, yielded corn crops, and the same was true with any other seeds.

Next, he explained that the amount of the yield or production would be determined by the care given and how much seed was planted. Thus, I would reap what I had sown according to care and the amount sown.

> But this I say, He which soweth sparingly shall reap also sparingly, and he which soweth bountifully shall reap also bountifully. Every man according as he purposeth in his heart, so let him give; not grudgingly,

"THE" DIET FOR YOUR MIND TO HELP YOU FIND THE TRUTH THAT WILL SET YOU FREE

or of necessity. for God loveth a cheerful giver. (II Corinthians 9:6-7)

The scripture, upon which the principle is founded, says you receive according to what you give. John and Bob are farmers, John plants five apple trees and Bob plants fifty trees. Each tree when reproducing normally will yield twenty apples. Hence, when harvest time comes, the results will be:

John – planted (gave) five apple trees, each of which yielded 20 apples; which is $5 \times 20 = 100$ apples.

Bob – planted (gave) 50 apple trees, each of which yielded 20 apples; which is $50 \times 20 = 1000$ apples.

Therefore, the point is, they received according to their giving. They reaped what they sowed. They planted apples. They did not reap bananas, or peaches, or corn; they reaped apples.

In love, some have been planting tares and expecting wheat, planting sparingly and expecting much; planting discord and expecting union; neglecting the planting and expecting it to yield on its own. Then when they reap according to their sowing, their overgrown egos burst forward blaming others, blaming God, or anyone other than himself or herself. When in truth, the self has several times before stood in this déjà vue. Did the self learn? No! No! No! Instead of realizing that all stems from the self; self experiences, education, environment, and so on, that is the diet of the mind, which sees with a mirror image, the self sought not to make the correction, but to complain and blame.

The effort here is to attempt to get each of us to look at ourselves. We should look not so much at what my mate or co-worker is or is not doing, as at what the self is doing or not doing. Remember the author of love, God, and God in the flesh. Jesus, taught, "Thou shalt love thou neighbor as thyself". (St. Matthew 22:39). Have I been only self-conscious and not placed my self-consciousness under the guidance of God-consciousness? Have I been true to others and myself according to the spiritual, or have I been seeing with selfish eyes? Is it possible that I have not (according to the scripture) practiced love? Do I need the truth that will make me free? Do I need to reprogram my mind, place it on a diet, because of the my high self-love cholesterol count?

We can conclude with the belief, according to our knowledge that this world, this nation, and the family would not exist if there were not love in each of them. Therefore, every now and then, take time out to think of life without love.

If we take love out of the world, then we would only have hatred and destruction.

If we take love out of a home cooked meal, we only have a restaurant.

If we take love out of work, we only have a job.

And if we take love out of romance, we are left with sex only.

This is why the world needs to understand and practice love. Most of the time in order to love, we have to seek in life's experiences not only the pleasures but also the experiences themselves. We must remember the expression, "No pain, No gain." It is the selfish self (the ego) that asks questions about what love has to do with it. Once you are born-again, there is another nature (spiritual) that actually lives within you. Thus, through the spirit, and only through the spirit, can we acknowledge the role that love plays in our lives, world, and existence. The self only knows the self and knows only how to love the self. The spirit is a part of all of us. Hence, through the spirit, we can love all. Through the physical, we hear the question. Through the spirit, we hear the answer: "love has everything to do with it because God is love."

BROTHERLY AND DIVINE LOVE

In the previous chapter, we noted that opposites are able to co-exist as one because they are able to give (love) to each other. Furthermore, this love is to be sought through the basic rule, "love thy neighbor as thyself."

We can never understand or practice loving others as ourselves until we have experienced the love of Jesus Christ. Through Him, by Him, and for Him, we understand loving thy neighbor as thyself.

When I was born anew (again), I was taken on a journey of my old self. The journey revealed my mistakes, my wrongdoings – against men and God. While traveling within my mind, after the spirit revealed all of my faults, it concluded with the highest, brightest, most welcome revelation. That revelation was that through it all, God through Jesus still loved me. At my worse moments of doing wrong to my fellow person, He was there all the time. At the worse moments of transgressions against God, Jesus was there all the time.

This experience, as I now reflect upon it, brings tears to my eyes. There was soul sorrowfulness, an awareness of giving, forgiving and understanding that cannot be described here or anywhere else. It is an experience that only those who have experienced the same can understand. Thus, when I came to the end of this spiritual journey, I was truly a new person. The experience was a revelation and the genesis of my new seeking to find the way, the truth, love and life. The need for a diet for my mind was recognized.

I then desired to know what love was. Thus, from that desire came the opening of the mind to the true self, the self that wanted so much to be like Jesus: loving (giving) when hurt, loving (forgiving) when wronged, loving (understanding) all things. Why I should give, why I should forgive, why I should understand – all was opened to me. This is where love has to begin. The selfish self learns to look to a greater (Godly) self and from a greater perspective it finds the truth that can help one learn how to love others.

Two Greek words are often used to explain love. These two are "eros" and "agape." Eros associates love with the physical, whereas agape has its origin in the spiritual.

Eros is the Greek god of love. Greek mythology, however, uses the word Eros to denote the strong physical attraction Paris feels for Helen and Zeus for Hera.[1]

Agape is the Greek word for love or charity. It often conveys the idea of a respectful and unselfish love, for example between parents and children or friends. It must have been chosen by the authors of the New Testament to avoid the implication of selfishness and passionate emotions often found in the usual word for love, eros.[2]

> This universality of love is founded on a new understanding of the relations between God and man revealed in Jesus Christ. God is not the God of only one people, but of the whole world. He "wants everyone to be saved." (1 Timothy 2.4) Since he "is love" (I John 4:8) "he loved so much the world that he gave His only Son so that everybody who believes in Him may have eternal life." (John 3.16) Jesus, His Son, manifested this love when "He loved his own to the end .. .laying down His life for them." (John 13:34) Such love, asking men to work for the fulfillment of the will of God for true happiness and the salvation of all men, cannot be a mere human love. It is possible because, "the love of God has been poured into our hearts by the Spirit given to us" (Romans 5:5), and it is the proof that we really love God and that His love is complete in us (I John 4:12) As principle and rule of the whole Christian life, it abides forever (I Corinthians 13).[3]

Thus, we find that even when considering love between persons, we must look to the love that is "agape" as opposed to the "eros." For eros has its beginning and ending in the physical.

The consistency of God is one of the fundamental reasons I have hope and trust in God. This awareness of His consistency came about through my becoming and developing a relationship through Jesus with God. Again, this consistency, which is the same yesterday, and today and forever, is what makes him truth. Thus, having grown tired of let downs by people, I needed to place my trust in a consistency.

"THE" DIET FOR YOUR MIND TO HELP YOU FIND THE TRUTH THAT WILL SET YOU FREE

Jesus in His divine mission, in His fulfillment of the law, took a step to help us understand the spirit of the law, which is consistent with the law of God. God gave Moses the law but the understanding of the law came from God through Jesus Christ.

The Pharisees and Sadducees – who taught that Jesus' teaching was in opposition to the law given through Moses – asked tricky questions of Jesus in the effort to trick Jesus and thereby substantiate their belief.

> The crowds were profoundly impressed by his answers – but not the Pharisees! When they heard that he had defeated the Sadducees with his reply, they thought up fresh questions of their own to ask Him. One of them, a lawyer, spoke up: "Sir, which is the most important command in the laws of Moses?" Jesus replied, "Love the Lord your God with all your heart, soul, and mind." This is the first and greatest commandment. The second most important is similar: "Love your neighbor as much as you love yourself." All the other commandments and all the demands of the prophets stem from these two laws and are fulfilled if you obey all the others. (St. Matthew 22:33-40 TLB)

In the twenty-ninth verse of chapter 22 of Matthew Jesus had told the Sadducees that they erred in knowledge and understanding of the scripture and we see the Pharisees doing the same thing. Furthermore, I wonder if they understood Jesus' answer about the great commandment in the law. Did they understand that the two commandments – love God and love thy neighbor as thyself – were really a summary of what the ten were all about? Did they know that the Ten Commandments are speaking of a dual relationship that we as humans have – a relationship of person to God, and a relationship of person to person? And how many people know this today? Hence, the ten can be divided into two parts. The first four commandments tell of the relationship God is requiring between a person and Him (God). The last six tell of the relationship we are to have, one to another.

TEN COMMANDMENTS
(ITS SUMMATION IN TWO COMMANDMENTS)

TEN COMMANDMENTS	RELATIONSHIPS	JESUS' SUMMARY
1. No God before Him 2. No graven Image 3. No taking of the Lord's name in vain 4. Remember the Sabbath Day to keep Holy	**PERSON TO GOD**	1–4. Love the Lord thy God with all your heart, soul and mind.
5. Honor your Father and Mother 6. You shall not kill 7. You shall not commit adultery 8. You shall not steal 9. You shall not lie to your neighbor 10. You shall not covet what your neighbor has	**PERSON TO PERSON**	5-10 Love your neighbor as much as you love yourself.

If we are to understand the two as a summary of the ten, we must examine the meaning(s) behind them.

A. BROTHERLY LOVE
(LOVE YOUR NEIGHBOR AS MUCH AS YOU LOVE YOURSELF)

Loving your neighbor as much as you love yourself means not doing anything to anyone else that you wouldn't want done to you. In other words, you wouldn't steal from someone because you wouldn't want anyone to steal from you. You wouldn't commit adultery because you would not want anyone to make love to your wife or

"THE" DIET FOR YOUR MIND TO HELP YOU FIND THE TRUTH THAT WILL SET YOU FREE

husband. You would not have the desire to kill anyone, because you wouldn't want to be killed and so on. We are not speaking here of refusing to do these acts because of the law of man, previously mentioned, but of refusing to do them because of love.

Brotherly love is when a man or a woman looks at another man or woman and sees that physically there may be a difference, but spiritually they are equal. ("For there is no respect of persons with God." Romans 2:11) One is able to look and see the unity of all life with the creator, God; one is able to look at another's faults and accept that individual because one recognizes that one also has faults and falls short in the Creator's eyes.

Often, I have shouted unfavorable remarks to other drivers because they had pulled into the street ahead of me, almost causing an accident. However, intentionally or unintentionally, I have pulled out ahead of an oncoming car. Now, I don't like listening to unfavorable remarks because of an error I made and I am sure that the same applies to the recipient of my unfavorable remarks. Realizing we all make errors, I have ceased making such remarks (almost).

The awakening of one's self to the unity of man and woman with God is the purpose of the scripture that says to love thy neighbor as thyself. This awakening will help you realize and say, "I am imperfect, I sin, and I make errors and wish to be accepted by others. Therefore, I will accept others with their errors." To love is to look beyond selfishness (self-consciousness) and find God-consciousness.

As a self-centered, self-conscious person, I want to receive forgiveness, end of story. As a Godly conscious person with a renewed mind, I want to receive forgiveness and give forgiveness because I realize that I should do unto others as I would have done to me.

You may say that these are evidences of love. What is love? When and where do we find love?

> Dear friends, let us practice loving each other, for love comes from God and those who are loving and kind show that they are the children of God, and that they are getting to know Him better. But if a person isn't loving and kind, it show's that he doesn't know God – for God is love. (I John 4:7—8 TLB)

The scripture found at I Corinthians 13 (the entire chapter) tells about love. However, as stated previously, the two types of love we are concerned with are love of God for man (divine love) and the love of person for another person (brotherly love).

Brotherly love was explained to be the recognition of the unity of life, which involves appreciating our fellow persons as much as we appreciate ourselves. If we are to answer the question "What, when and where is love?" we must turn to the Holy Bible. The above quoted scripture tells us that God is love. Therefore, love is spiritual in nature and is found within oneself, when one loves others and God.

Thus, we can conclude that Brotherly love is giving to fellow persons, forgiving fellow persons and seeking the understanding of fellow persons. We can also conclude that this approach is the only way to remove the separation of persons and to reunite persons. Then we come to realize that sin not only causes a separation of humanity from God, but also causes separation within humanity. Humanity after eating the forbidden fruit started seeing with the physical eye the differences, which led to the appearance of differences. It also led humanity to start accusing one another.

However, when sin is washed away with the blood of Jesus, persons can see with the sixth sense and with a mind that has followed a diet. Then with the sixth sense, a derivative of the Spirit-filled mind that has followed a diet, the person can see that if there is to be a reuniting of humanity, we need giving, forgiving and a holy understanding. A mind on a diet of the spiritual brings the truth that it is what's inside that matters. The pecan can be used here to further understand the importance of the inside over the outside.

It is the core, the meat of the pecan, that matters. The pecan may come in a variety of shapes, sizes and colors, but the inside is what the pecan is about. So, whether the pecan is long or short in size, or light or dark in color, each has its individual meat.

That's the way it is with humanity, as with the pecan. Although, the meat of humanity is the soul and spirit of the person, still it's what's inside, the intangible unseen, that is of importance.

The accusing of one another is another sign of the lack of brotherly love. Again, the accusing began with Adam and Eve, after they ate of the forbidden fruit. Their notice of differences led to the fig-leaf clothing. Then, when questioned about the eating of the forbidden fruit, Adam accused Eve and Eve accused the serpent and the serpent accused all humanity. God in recognizing the separation made the commandment that persons are to love one another.

B. DIVINE LOVE
(LOVING GOD)

The first commandment Jesus mentioned was, "Love the Lord your God with all your heart, soul, and mind." (This was a call for divine love). What did Jesus mean when He made these remarks? He was and is saying that to love the Lord with all your mind is to think of God constantly, to put Him first in everything; to apply thoughts of God in everything we do. These thoughts will accord with what the Bible says should be our attitude towards one another, God and to ourselves. The mind is the creator of ideas. Thus, when we think of God, our ideas will be those of a Godly nature. To love the Lord with our minds is to look to God to guide us, to look to God and trust Him. Regardless of the circumstances we face, our minds must remain intact with God; we must do as He would have us do.

The mind is on the one true God, the God of Isaac and Jacob. The mind accepts only the true God; no other is before or after Him. We have no images to recognize God; we can only worship Him in Spirit. Our minds never say anything that would blaspheme the name of God. Our minds recognize that six days the Lord worked and the seventh (Sabbath), He rested. Hence, we will give our minds a day of rest from the toil and stress of this physical life, to think and do the things that are of God.

To love the Lord with our souls is to allow God's ideas or purpose for anything under our control to be carried out regardless of the sacrifices that may have to be made. We look within our inner selves and find the spirit that God has manifested within us. Loving our souls is finding the nature of God (the creator) and allowing his nature to mature and unfold. The soul has reference to that which is the core of all existence. Thus, loving from the core will certainly produce from the core. Only through God can we find the strength to do the things of God.

BROTHERLY AND DIVINE LOVE

To love the Lord within our hearts is to let God live inside our hearts. Thus, then and only then can we give to God or a person, forgive God or a person and understand God or a person. (Please see the chapter on the Essence of Love.)

To love the Lord with all our heart is to feel and have compassion for your fellow person as God has for you. Well, you say that is brotherly love. Yes, it is brotherly love, but remember the only way to have brotherly love is to have divine love. They are reciprocals of each other. It is like a mirror. An object exists and the image is reflected in the mirror. If nothing is placed before the mirror, nothing is reflected. Therefore, if you love God, you will love your fellow person. If you love your fellowman, you will love God: for this indeed is how we show love.

The following scripture will support the truth that to love God is to love your fellow person.

> If a man say, I love God, and hateth his brother, he is a liar: for he that loveth not his brother whom he hath seen, how can he love God, whom he had not seen? And this commandment have we from Him, That he who loveth God loveth his brother also. (I John 4:20-21)

Finally, when we speak of loving God and loving our neighbor, we are saying that according to God and as spoken by Jesus; to be obedient to God, to follow Jesus, there must be a dual relationship. Each individual must have a relationship with God and relationships with other individuals. We stated above that the reason Jesus came was to reunite, or reestablish the relationship of person to God and now we further see His coming was also to reestablish the person-to-person relationship.

Thus, we could say there has to be a vertical as well as a horizontal relationship. The vertical would be the individual's reaching out to establish a rapport with God. This rapport will cause a person to serve and worship the Lord in spirit and truth.

> But the hour cometh, and now is, when the true worshippers shall worship the Father in spirit and truth: for the Father seeketh such to worship Him. (St. John 4:23)

"THE" DIET FOR YOUR MIND TO HELP YOU FIND THE TRUTH THAT WILL SET YOU FREE

In true worship of God, we find the sister to worship, which is service – service to God. Hence, in conjunction with worship there is service. Often I have seen signs over church entrances or in church bulletins that read, "Enter to Worship. Depart to Serve."

> My worship of God is first and foremost, far above and beyond my work or service. God did not save us just to serve as we so often hear. He saved us to love us and to be loved by us. But how do we love God? How do we serve God and work? And how do we express this love? We do this by serving one another. We have two relationships – a vertical one with worship and a horizontal one with service. Unless my horizontal relationship with others is right, my worship isn't going to mean much. If our worship is only in word but not in deed (as Jesus says), then we short-circuit our worship.[4]

In my attempt to communicate, through a sermon, the importance of helping one another, I use a truth that I hope to be a revelation of understanding service to one another. This truth is that God has always used humans, like ourselves, to help us understand the true God.

There was Noah, to whom God spoke, to tell the people about the coming flood. There were Abraham and Sarah, who would be the father and mother of a nation called God's chosen people. There were prophets – Isaiah, Jeremiah, Ezekiel and others – used by God to speak to the nation of God's chosen people. When this nation was in need, God supplied them by means of a prophet or chosen individual. Moses was used by God to bring the nation out of captivity.

Yes, God in the past – and today – uses persons here on earth to help others. God is consistent. God is the same yesterday, today, and tomorrow. His methods may change, but He is the same. And the use of persons to help persons is one method He has not changed.

Therefore, when God is ready to help you or me, a friend or an enemy, He will not fly down in a Concord or a 747. God will not drive up to our door in a Rolls Royce or a Volkswagen. What God will do is send a person to be used by Him to help a saint or sinner. Thus, this is how we serve God. We serve God by serving our neighbor, a fellow person, man or woman. Hence, if we love God, we will serve God. Therefore, to serve God, we attend to the needs of one another.

And I, the King, will tell them, 'When you did it to these my brothers you were doing it to me!'(St. Matthew *25:40TLB)* (Please read Verses 31-46)

MALE-FEMALE! HUSBAND-WIFE! AND LOVE

We have established that true love is based in the spiritual. However, when two beings, opposite by nature, attempt to become one, attempt on the physical plane to feel earthquakes, a tickling in the toes, a weakness in the knees, and want to be Godly sure they are hearing church bells and not school bells; what fruit (you will know a tree by its fruit) should they expect to find? I've gotten my mind together. I want to know what I should look for in a relationship; what are the signs, of true love – love of an agape nature but carried out on the eros plane.

You must always look at other persons for their spiritual qualities. If one's spiritual nature is not acknowledged and awakened, one is not of God. Yet, with this recognition you will still decide to pursue another on the basis of physical attractiveness, or some other superficial (physical) appearance. That is your masochistic business. However, if you desire to find qualities in an opposite, with the desire to love another and have that love reciprocated, then God has given us a further glance into love.

A professor, who taught in the theological seminary I attended, put into a formula what the pastoral ministry should be concerned with when counseling is given prior to marriage. Since love is the reason people are led to marriage, I believe the formula is appropriate here.

The formula that the professor gave contains five elements. The five elements are: 1) Friendship; 2) Frankness; 3) Fidelity; 4) Forgiveness; and 5) Faith.

1-FRIENDSHIP (SOUL-MATE)

Sometime ago, I was visiting a friend who had a married couple as guests. I was questioned as to what kind of woman I would like to marry. I was asked what is most important for me to find in a woman.

MALE-FEMALE! HUSBAND-WIFE! AND LOVE

I immediately answered, "A friend." Being a Christian, I went on to say why I believe a friend is what I wanted in the person who would not be my equal, nor my superior or subordinate, who would be no more twain, but a part of me.

> And the rib, which the Lord God had taken from man, made he a woman, and brought her unto the man. And Adam said, This is now bone of my bones, and flesh of my flesh: she shall be called Woman, because she was taken out of Man. Therefore shall a man leave his father and his mother, and shall be one flesh. (Genesis 2:22-24)

The part of me, which the mate would become would be flesh of my flesh; after all we all are descendants of Adam and Eve and more. This mate would be a "soul-mate". However, since the expression "soul-mate" has been misused and abused in the same way as love and has become an everyday expression of the physical world, I will venture into why I say "soul- mate" and what a "soul-mate" is to me.

Webster states a soul-mate is a person temperamentally suited to another. To me, a "soul-mate" is a person who has been born-again. Then the heart of the mate is under the guidance of the Godly consciousness, or the Spirit and will of God. I will say it now and again later, that because the Spirit of God is in control, my soul-mate and I will not have a relationship in her way, because she is woman, or in my way because I am a man, but a relationship in Jesus' way. After all, He made the humanity that became a living soul. Thus, only by the two of us being born-again can we even begin to become temperamentally suited to one another.

A soul-mate will always look to the spirit and not the physical. A mate realizes that physically she and I may be different. However, in the Spirit, we are the same. The mate will be constantly reminded that Jesus has the right to say His way because He made the mate and me. As Genesis says, when Adam (the man) and Eve (the woman) were created they were as one without any shame. It was the awakening of the consciousness that led to the separation of man and woman. Thus, through Christ and only through Christ can there be a relationship of a woman and man. Through Christ they can return and re-establish the unity that existed before the disobedience of Adam and Eve. This unity was founded upon the Spirit of God. Thus, He came and died for this possible reuniting. This is the second reason why he has a right to say His way is the true way.

> Jesus said, "Greater love hath no man than this, that a man lay down his life for his friends." (St. John 15:13)
>
> For Christ entered into heaven itself, to appear now before God as our friend. (Hebrew 9:24 TLB)

Jesus is a Christian's greatest friend, so when it comes to a mate, the closest we can get to marrying Jesus is to marry a fellow Christian.

A friend is defined as: 1) a person whom one knows well and is fond of; and 2) an ally, supporter, or sympathizer. An ally is a country or person joined with another for a common purpose.

Webster's goes on to say a friend is one attached to another by affection or esteem, one that is not hostile, one that is of the same nation, party, or group.

These definitions give an abstract idea of a friend, but I would like to share common traits in interactions with a friend. In the relationships between a man and a woman, a friend is the person you can call on at any time for a favor, a deed, an open ear, an open heart, and an open purse. Of course, the same is reciprocated. A friend is not one who tells you that you are right when you are wrong or who agrees to everything (for the sake of acceptance). Thus, a friend gives only the advice that he or she would give himself or herself (love thy neighbor as thyself). The advice could be hard to swallow or lead to a path where the other may not wish to go. However, all things are done for the growth of one another.

In your life experiences, how many times have you been told by a "friend" what to do or not to do only to see this "friend" doing what he or she advised you against. You hear a friend say, "Man, I wouldn't accept her if she doesn't listen to me," only to find that his girl or wife has only to snap her fingers and he comes running. Or, you hear the lady say, "Girl, I wouldn't take that off of him," when in fact she takes things which are worse from her man. The point is that a friend who is like a mother (defending the child when wrong) and who never seeks truth and understanding is not a friend, but the contributor to a selfish spoiled brat.

The abstract definitions do not truly supply a total definition. The attempt through common experience to understand what a friend should be is also falling short. Hence, we return to the scripture for a further and Holy understanding. The scriptures say, "A friend loveth at all times..." (Proverbs 17.9) So, we are back to love (giving, forgiving, and understanding). The two people must love each other to be friends. If they each understand love, how to practice love, and put love into action, then they each have a friend. I know because, as I said above, Jesus is my best friend and He taught me how to love. Giving is in His nature. Remember, there can be no greater giving than when a person gives his life for a friend, and He did just that.

Even though a friend may be different, the two of you have a number of things in common. Your various ideas are basically the same.

Recently my biological mother went to the bosom of Abraham. The family decided that I would give the eulogy at her going home assembly. Above I mentioned that when God desires to help a person He would send another person to help the person in need. Well, God sent me a friend I call Jesus. He also sent a friend that some called Ola, Sis. Settle, and other names. You know what I called her; I called her my second best friend, second only to Jesus Christ. I called her mom.

The subject of the eulogy was, "My Two Best Friends: my friend Ola and my friend Jesus." My friend Ola gave me my first birth and my friend Jesus gave me my second birth. My friend Jesus gave me the Word, the Word of truth. My friend Ola taught me to seek the Word, study the Word and carry the Word with me everywhere I go. She gave me the Holy understanding of the Word.

Mom was a friend that had her own opinion but who loved me even when her opinion wasn't victorious. An example would be when I was ten and I expressed to her my desire to become a lawyer, an attorney at law. Mom would often reply, "Son, why do you want to be a lawyer? Everybody says they are crooks and liars. You are a good son, but people will think that you are a liar and a crook." However, she would never stop on that negative. She would go on to say, "But son, if a lawyer is what you want to be, I'll support you as much as I can."

Mom was truly a friend. There are many other examples I could give to substantiate her true friendship and love. However, the purpose here is to show an example of true love and friendship.

Friends must spend time together and enjoy spending time together. They must not only love one another but also like each other. Most of us have been programmed with the "first impression is the lasting impression" attitude. Whether we are seeking employment, an associate or a mate, we have been programmed to do certain things to be accepted; this is commonly referred to as putting your best foot forward. The above was mentioned to show how a person, in an effort to win another's acceptance, will say what they think the other person wants to hear, and do what they believe the other person wants them to do. There is nothing wrong with displaying your best clothes, cologne and manners when a relationship is initiated. However, too often, two individuals fail to accomplish a sound relationship or a good marriage, because both are pretending to be something other than themselves. Hence, after the novelty of the relationship wears off, when the real him or the real her surfaces, after the thrill seems to leave the marriage, then the two that were one, once again become two.

2-FRANKNESS

Pretending to be a person that you are not leads to a trained mind. This is a mind that causes you to forget to be for real. Even though the '70s had the label, "Do your own thing," people couldn't because they didn't know what their own thing was. So, even their own thing could not bring them to be frank and honest with each other. This is the second element needed, frankness. Frankness in all communications, body language and oral language must be included. Each must be able to approach the other with their true feelings on and in all matters if the two are to exist as one. One caveat should be taken into consideration. Communications, if we want them to be open and true, must not be rooted in the "I'm right and you are wrong" type of attitude or a biased or judgmental attitude.

There is a possibility that both may be right. Even a stopped clock is right twice a day. However, what has to be determined is what is best for the couple. We should consider the "we" and not the "I." Oh, they may disagree on certain topics. When there is earnest communication, disagreement surfaces. However, if the attitude of "who will win?" enters the discussion (from either party), the result will be nobody will win, because the approach is based on adversity and winning as opposed to understanding. Therefore, what's best is not sought. The couple seeks only to discover how miserable they can make each other.

For example, the husband consistently leaves the shower on after use. When the wife enters, in a rush to get dressed, and turns on the water, instead of the water coming out into the tub, it comes out of the shower wetting her hair. Thus, her hair gets wet and is a mess. She shouts out to the husband that she has requested several times in the past that he turn the shower off after use. However, he continues to do the same. Her previous requests have been ignored. He shouts back that she could have checked the shower before entering. Then the volley of shouting begins. Thus, instead of trying to understand one another, trying to make adjustments, which are needed when two come together, they lash out after one another. Both are seeking to be a winner, neither is seeking to be a friend.

Throughout this writing, "to love" has been defined as "to give, to forgive through understanding." In *Love, Power and Justice,*[1] Paul Thillich would say that "to love" is "to give, forgive and listen." As Jesus would often say after stating a parable, "Those who have ears let them hear." If we expect and desire another person to be open and frank with us, we must listen and try to understand. If one is to understand, one must listen. One must not listen with a prejudicial ear, a judgmental ear, or a precocious ear. The listening has to be with an objective ear, not a subjective ear. Listen with the desire to give, the desire to forgive, because you desire to understand. Yes, it's so simple in theory, but because of mind programming, we find it difficult in practice. Now we have learned that we can reprogram the mind (renew the mind) by placing it on a diet. We know it's possible to take the theory and turn the theory into reality.

"THE" DIET FOR YOUR MIND TO HELP YOU FIND THE TRUTH THAT WILL SET YOU FREE

Another result of phoniness, instead of frankness, is that a person fails to express their true feelings. Thus each time the agitating thing takes place, the truth is buried. Hence, the other person is not aware that they are in the wrong. Jesus said that nothing will be hidden that will not come to light. Indeed, He tells the truth because the little problems eventually escalate into larger ones. Thus, instead of getting closer, people drift apart. Most of the time they do it without really knowing why.

When I practiced law, as a private attorney, many married persons sat across from my desk and stated that their spouse had changed. Meanwhile the spouse would say that he or she had not changed. My conclusion was that they didn't know one another from the beginning. Not only was there phoniness in the relationship, but also love was indeed blind. Each saw in the other what he or she wanted to see. Often we hear, "If you love me then you will accept me as I am." Using the Bible as their source, people use the statement that Jesus accepts us just as we are. Hence, who are you to find fault? Yes, Jesus does accept us just as we are. However, when that acceptance is received, we are born-again, born of the Spirit. And Christ expects us each day through His word, actions and experiences to change, to grow, to become more like Him.

The same is true in relationships. I don't need a female who doesn't desire to try to help me to be better tomorrow than I am today. And I would understand losing someone if I couldn't help her to change. So, why would a person want to be with another person and there is no growth for either after a year (356 days) has passed?

"Well," you may say, "did we not previously say that what makes Jesus the truth is that He's the same yesterday, today and tomorrow (forever)? Then why can't I remain the same?" The answer can be found in Holy understanding. We start with Holy understanding, which is the recognition of the fall of humanity from grace. The eating of the forbidden fruit caused the need to seek a spiritual diet of the Word. The spiritual diet is needed to "change" the dieter's mind into a mind like Christ's.

> Let this mind be in you, which was also in Christ Jesus: (Philippians 2:5)

MALE-FEMALE! HUSBAND-WIFE! AND LOVE

So, since we are on a mind diet, during our entire life, to be like Christ, we should be growing or changing. Therefore, we shouldn't be the same today as yesterday and even more changes should occur by tomorrow.

Yes, I would accept her as she is, and I desire the same of her. However, if we are not growing, we (the relationship) will surely die. Furthermore, if changes are needed, and they certainly will when opposites come together, they will occur through frank communication. This communication may include criticism. If it's earnest criticism, if each party is free to give as well as receive criticism, and the object is not to win but to understand, the criticism – if accepted – will be for the good. This criticism is earnest and constructive.

When I entered the ministry, I had a habit of reading the scriptures too fast. When I asked a friend for constructive criticism, she would always say, "You did well, but you read the scriptures too fast and it's hard to understand what you are saying." Of course, I could have told her she was a layperson and therefore she could not criticize me as a minister. However, even though my ego was initially involved, I viewed her criticism as being rooted in love, concern for my growth. Because of her interest to see me do better and because of my recognizing it, she always would say, "I am not doing this to hurt you, but rather to help your ministry." I listened, not adversely or defensively, but with an open ear to her criticism. Hence, later my pastor would often tell me how much he and the members enjoyed listening to my reading of the scriptures.

There is another consideration that needs to be observed. If a person in a relationship, before or during marriage, finds that the differences with the other person are beyond a mere adjusting, then maybe the Holy understanding is that you don't belong together. No, I am not advocating divorce. Nor am I supporting a speedy separation. However, what I am advocating is co-existence in harmony.

We can readily understand the principle of uneven yoke. The theory is that a Christian should not be seeking a marriage with a non-Christian. However, with the uneven yoke comes the need for the holy understanding of the knowledge of whom God intends to have

"THE" DIET FOR YOUR MIND TO HELP YOU FIND THE TRUTH THAT WILL SET YOU FREE

you joined together with. This knowledge will bring with it the assurance that no one can ever set you and your mate apart.

> What therefore God hath joined together, let no man put asunder. (St. Mark 10:9)

Thus comes the understanding that because two persons are Christians, their relationship is not automatically placed into the protection of God. This is because God made each of his children as individuals. So when the person is born-again he or she carries his or her individuality. This means all Christians are not identical in character. If we study the behavior of Peter, one of Jesus' disciples, we'll find a fiery, aggressive out-spoken individual, whereas, the disciple John is reported to have been gentle, compassionate, and passive.

The two, Peter and John, were both chosen by Jesus to be His disciples. Yet, their characteristics were as different as their names. Yet, Jesus saw how both were needed in the work of the Kingdom of God. We could say that Peter's characteristics resembled the Father's, a character of power, courage and strength. John's character was that of love, giving, forgiving and understanding, the same as Jesus. So, since the Christian community is made up of different personalities, when a soul-mate is sought there must be a true revealing of one's self.

When it comes to persons sharing a relationship of intimacy, especially marriage, there has to be like and love for there to be harmony in their co-existing. Previously we said that one of the problems in co-existing as humans is that people get liking mixed up with loving. Now that you understand the difference you also understand that you can have both and both are needed when you are choosing a mate. In the physical or flesh, liking is confused with loving. In the spiritual, with a born-again renewed mind, liking is understood to be not a lesser degree of loving, but rather a complement to agape love which enhances the erotic (in marriage) love.

Yes, we said differences can co-exist and often are co-dependent on one another. We have discussed man and plant as well as man and woman co-existing. Music has been used to further illustrate the differences co-existing in harmony. Again I will use the elements of music to illustrate a point. The "A" note will bring harmony and unison when used in a "C" chord, whereas in an "F" chord the "A" note will echo disharmony. What is being said is that after you find a person you believe to be a friend and you are open to having a mate, you must be able to be frank with the person. The person and you must have a number of things in common. So, when you are being earnest and frank with him or her, that person knows that you are an "A" note. Therefore, if he or she is an "F" chord both of you will have a holy understanding of the disharmony that lies ahead. In other words, the holy understanding will lead you to the note that is compatible to your note. Furthermore, all born-again believers are children of God, but some are "A" or "B" notes and work well in certain chords. The key to being able to be friends and frank with one another is to first know which note you are: "A," "B," "C," "D," "E" or "F" and then which note will work in harmony with your note.

Please remember to be true to thine own self. Thus, an "A" note is an "A" note, whether it is played on a string or wind instrument. A musician can distinguish the "A" note from the "C" note in the musical world. Well, with a mind on the spiritual diet you can distinguish (discern) "A" and "C" notes in the spiritual world.

Yes, for a marriage, or a relationship that develops into marriage, to grow and continue, there must be frankness between the parties involved.

3-FIDELITY

The third essential element is *fidelity*. Thus, immediately we think of fidelity as being the absence of another sexual partner in the relationship. However, when infidelity is explored we find that the third party usually enters the picture because of the failure on the part of one or both parties to be a friend and have frankness in their relationship. Therefore, what is missing is sought and found elsewhere, thereby leading to a deterioration of the relationship. However, with the seeking of the first two elements – friendship and frankness – mentioned above, the third party entrance is blocked with a love thick door.

"THE" DIET FOR YOUR MIND TO HELP YOU FIND THE TRUTH THAT WILL SET YOU FREE

    Fidelity in love, or between two persons, does not only exclude a third sexual partner, but also excludes any other thing (profession) or person (child) that becomes an alternative or distraction to the spouse or partner. The alternative and distraction are found when: a person is willing to give more time to a career or profession than to their mate or when a child's needs are met, but not the husband's or when the husband's time is spent at the office and the wife is left at home alone. So, persons (other sexual partners and/or children) and careers can stifle the relationship and cause the one who is neglected to seek other outlets.

    In any relationship there must be a continuous concern that nothing, save God, comes before one another. In the church, I find many husbands getting angry with their wives because they are at the church building so often. This loyalty on the part of the wife to God is what the husband sees as an opposition to their marriage. However, for the most part, the husbands who do not accept this loyalty, are not in the church themselves, so they don't understand. Furthermore, words written here will do little more than enunciate a problem. Until these husbands (and sometimes wives) have a renewing of their mind toward God, nothing said to them will justify the other's church-going behavior. But, as stated, friendship requires having things in common. It requires frankness and creates the need to understand one another. Fidelity begins with the relationship being evenly yoked.

> Be ye not unequally yoked together with believers: for what fellowship hath righteousness with unrighteousness? and what communion hath light with darkness? And what concord hath Christ with Belial? or what part hath he that believeth with an infidel? And what agreement hath the temple of God with idols? for ye are the temple of the living God, as God hath said, I will dwell in them, and walk in them, and I will be their God, and they shall be my people. Wherefore come out from among them, and be ye separate, saith the Lord, and touch not the unclean thing; and I will receive you, And will be a Father unto you, and ye shall be my sons and daughters, saith the Lord Almighty. (II Corinthians 6:14-18)

MALE-FEMALE! HUSBAND-WIFE! AND LOVE

Often in the church, a saved person marries an unsaved person. The scripture which says, "Come ye out from among them," is ignored. Sooner or later they will come out from among each other because their thought pattern (mind programming) is rooted in opposition. A child of God's philosophy or way of life is "do unto others as you would have them do unto you." Whereas, the way of life for a child of the world is: "do unto others before they do unto you."

Note that the world has no written word to be guided by. It's whatever, whenever, however, with whomever. They can strike at the ball ten times and not be out. They can lie to you each and every time and not be held consciously responsible.

When man and woman, who are capable of thinking and doing everything on their own, which includes acting on a selfish attitude, attempt to come together as one, they will find success only through a medium. The best medium I know is Jesus. Things must be not his way, not her way, but Jesus' way. This leaves each with a feeling of the other having an input but not domination in the relationship. Thus for guidance in the relationship, Jesus is used as the medium. So, if you are interested in a person who is not in the church, and you are in the church, then let God save him or her before you walk down the aisle. If you are married to an unsaved person, then turn him or her, in prayer, over to the Lord. If you both are not saved, not in the church, then if you have problems that seem to be unsolvable, before you take the common approach (divorce), give God a try. Remember that if the relationship is to continue, it must have love. Again, the scripture says God is love. Hence, when you receive God, both of you will receive the potential to love. Thus, it is through and from His love that the two of you can learn to love.

The root of many infidelities can be traced to people seeking something from someone other than their mate. May I suggest that you seek all of your needs through and in Christ. If you need to feel appreciated, Jesus will show you your worth. If you need a lover, Jesus is love. How can these occurrences actually happen? Remember, when we have a need, God through Christ who lives in us (who are born-again) will work through one of us to supply the need. You see, it's not always finding another or the right person as much as it is finding the right source. Hence, when God is your source, the right person is provided through His wisdom and knowledge. Furthermore, you will have a built-in fix-it resource. Since God was the source in bringing the relationship or marriage together, God will fix any problem in the same. God is like any creator. He repairs and brings to the creation according to its needs.

Christians who are married or who anticipate marriage, and who believe that God through Christ has brought the two of them together, will find great assurance and comfort in the scriptures that say God is the author of marriage.

> "Don't you read the scriptures?" he replied. "In them it is written that at the beginning God created man and woman, and that a man should leave his father and mother, and be forever united to his wife. The two shall become one – no longer two, but one. And no man may divorce what God has joined together." (St. Matthew 19:4-6 TLB)

God's word (the Manual) is the genesis, the rock upon which we Christians build our trust, hope and faith. We know from His word that He must be true to the same. Additional assurances are found in other scriptures.

> "I also tell you this—if two of you agree down here on earth concerning anything you ask for, my Father in heaven will do it for you. For where two or three are gathered because they are mine, I will be right there among them." (St. Matthew 18:19-20 TLB)

The marriage is rooted in the knowledge that God through Christ has brought the parties together. Earnest prayer has been uttered to the heavenly Father with the request that His will be done. Therefore, God made (or will make) the marriage and God will take care of the marriage. When there is a problem, infidelity or otherwise, either or both parties can take the problem to God through Christ. Thus, He who made the partnership (marriage) will assist in eliminating the problem.

To further assist in God's involvement with the marriage, we can reexamine some common experiences previously mentioned. When you have a problem (malfunction) with your RCA television, to whom do you take it for repairs? RCA, right? When your Buick car

MALE-FEMALE! HUSBAND-WIFE! AND LOVE

has need of repair, you don't carry it to Ford or Toyota. You return it to Buick. Buick or RCA created their respective products and are the best sources to identify and rectify the problem. The same is true with marriage created or made by God. He made it. Hence, if something is wrong with it, He knows what's best to fix it. Furthermore, what is joined in the name of Jesus will remain.

Therefore, regardless of the problem or its nature, God will know what to do. Hence, if you have not previously done so, please allow God to take care of your marriage or anticipated marriage. Moreover, this third party (God through Jesus) will not cause or allow infidelity, but rather fidelity.

4-FORGIVENESS

The fourth element needed in the relationship is *forgiveness,* the ability of both partners to forgive one another for trespasses. The previous discussion on the need for forgiveness and what forgiveness is about will serve as the beginning of understanding forgiveness. Hence, both partners must recognize this need and put the same into practice.

One problem I've found in many marriages and relationships is the inability to forgive. There may be giving, but whether there is forgiving is questionable. This is based upon the large number of divorces. The failure of a person to put up with things from their spouse as they would outsiders has led many to a double standard.

Sometime ago I discussed with a friend the two faces of most of us. There is the face that we project or wear at work or with the public. Then there is the face we wear at home. The former finds us attempting to show a smile, lending an ear, or just trying to be pleasant. The latter face is less tolerant, less patient and less sensitive. We will forgive a co-worker but hold a grudge against the one we supposedly love. Yet, we say we love our spouses and they are supposedly more valuable. If we forgive grudgingly, with resentment, do we truly forgive? Or, do we follow the advice, "Don't get angry, get even."

The question with reference to forgiving is raised because many have adopted the above advice and approach. Hence, we claim that we love, whereas in fact we actually do not forgive. We find more satisfaction in getting even than forgiving.

Dorothy and Mack have been married for ten years. Around the seventh year, Dorothy was faced with Mack's infidelity. They separated for several weeks. Nevertheless, Mack was taken back into the house and the family remained intact; at least Mack believed it did. Little did he know that Dorothy had begun her get-even activities. Mack had noticed a change in her behavior – a lack of affection and attention. Oh, she cooked, worked, cared for the children as a loving parent and wife, but there was something different in their relationship. Naturally he attributed the change to his infidelity and hoped that time would mend her heart and their marriage. However, Dorothy had not and would not forgive Mack and sought to pay him back. Her statement to friends was, "I'll never forgive him."

To forgive means to give up wanting to punish and thereby pardon the act and the individual who performed the act. To get even negates the pardoning and forgiving and adds to a speedy journey down the road of destruction (divorce in marriage and separation in friendship).

If a marriage, a friendship or any type of partnership is to exist, then we must pardon the individual and the individual's acts that offend or injure. This pardoning is called forgiving. Remember we are followers of Christ and Jesus taught us to incorporate forgiveness into our co-existence with one another. Not only did he incorporate forgiving into person-to-person relationships, but he started with incorporating forgiving into the person-to-God relationship.

Is it not true that a person only has access to God because God through Christ has forgiven the person of their sins?

> In fact we can say that under the old agreement almost everything was cleansed by sprinkling it with blood. and without the shedding of blood there is no forgiveness of sins. (Hebrews 9:22 TLB)
>
> He cancels the first system in favor of a far better one. Under the new plan we have been forgiven and made clean by Christ's dying for us once and for all. (Hebrews 10:9-10 TLB)
>
> But Christ gave himself to God for our sins as one sacrifice for all time, and then sat down in the place of

MALE-FEMALE! HUSBAND-WIFE! AND LOVE

> highest honor at God's right hand, waiting for his enemies to be laid under his feet. (Hebrews 10:12-13 TLB)

Isn't it true that without the forgiving of sin there is a separation of man from God? Also, is it not the truth that sin separates, but love reconciles man back to God? Then doesn't it stand to reason that the part of love that is essential is forgiving? After all, if Jesus had not given his life that we would be forgiven of our sins, we would have no advocate or representative in heaven with the right to allow us to the tree of life.

> Therefore if any man be in Christ, he is a new creature: old things are passed away; behold, all things are become new. And all things are of God, who hath reconciled us to himself by Jesus Christ, and hath given to us the ministry of reconciliation; To wit, that God was in Christ, reconciling the world unto himself, not imputing their trespasses unto them; and hath committed unto us the word of reconciliation. (II Corinthians 5:17-19)

The need for forgiveness is essential in the person-to-person relationship as well as in the person-to-God relationship.

There is a story in the Manual about a man named Jacob (also known as Israel) and one of Jacob's sons, Joseph.

> Now Israel loved Joseph more than all his children, because he was the son of his old age; and he made him a coat of many colors. And when his brethren saw that their father loved him more than all of his brethren, they hated him, and could not speak peaceably unto him. And Joseph dreamed, and he told it his brethren: and they hated him yet the more. And he said unto them, Hear, I pray you, this dream which I have dreamed: For behold, we were binding sheaves in the field, and, lo, my sheaf arose, and also stood upright; and. Behold, your sheaves stood round about, and made obeisance to my sheaf. And his brethren said to him, Shalt thou indeed reign over us? Or shalt thou indeed have dominion over us? And they hated him yet

the more for his dreams, and for his words. (Genesis 37:3-8)

And his brethren went to feed the their father's flock in Shechem. And he said to him, Go, I pray thee, see whether it be well with thy brethren, and well with the flock; and bring me word again.

And when they saw him afar off, even before he came near unto them, they conspired against him to slay him.

And it came to pass when Joseph was come unto his brethren, that they stript Joseph out of his coat, his coat of many colours that was on him; And they took him, and cast him into a pit: and the pit was empty, there was no water in it. And they sat down to eat bread: and they lifted up their eyes and looked, and, behold, a company of Ishmeelites came from Gilead with their camels bearing spicery and balm and myrrh, going to carry it down to Egypt. And Judah said unto his brethren, What profit is it if we slay our brother, and conceal his blood? Come, and let us sell him to the Ishmeelites, and let not our hand be upon him: for he is our brother and our flesh. And his brethren were content. Then there passed by Midianites merchantmen; and they drew and lifted up Joseph out of the pit, and sold Joseph to the Ishmeelites for twenty pieces of silver: and they brought Joseph into Egypt. (Genesis 37:12-14, 18, 23-28)

The story goes on to tell how Joseph's brothers lied to their father that an animal killed Joseph. Then Jacob, their father, died. The brothers felt that since the father was no longer present to be a buffer between them and Joseph, who had become ruler over his brothers, that Joseph would seek revenge. However, the Manual says Joseph had a forgiving spirit.

And Joseph returned into Egypt, he, and his brethren, and all that went up with him to bury his father, after he had buried his father. And when Joseph brethren saw that their father was dead, they said,

Joseph will peradventure hate us, and will certainly requite us all the evil which we did unto him. And they sent a messenger unto Joseph, saying, Thy father did command before he died, saying, So shall ye say unto Joseph, Forgive, I pray thee now, the trespass of thy brethren, and their sin; for they did unto thee evil: and now, we pray forgive the trespass of the servants of the God of thy father. And Joseph wept when they spake unto him. And his brethren also went and fell down before his face; and they said, Behold, we be thy servants. And Joseph said unto them, Fear not: for am I in the place of God? But as for you, ye thought evil against me; but God meant it unto good, to bring to pass, as it is this day, to save much people alive. Now therefore fear ye not: I will nourish you, and your little ones. And he comforted them, and spake kindly unto them. (Genesis 50:14-21)

The above tells a part of the life of a God-fearing man. Joseph is one of the few individuals mentioned in the Manual who had few if any flaws. Joseph by his approach to his brethren has shown us that as persons we are to forgive other persons who have done us wrong.

You may say that this is an example of a family. Where in the manual can I find a person forgiving another when there is no biological relationship? Well above when the definition of love was being presented, it is stated that we should forgive our brother, not necessary a biological, but rather the universal brother, of his seven times a day trespasses, seven times a day. In other words, we should forgive others as forgiving is needed. We forgive because we want God and persons to forgive us of our trespasses.

This is especially true in relationships, which include marriage. The element of love – forgiving – has to be present. Anyway, isn't it true that one of the main reasons we want to get married to a person is because of love? Oh, you mean libido and not agape love.

Now you see why libido, or erotic love, will not survive without agape love. Again we are reminded that it's the spirit of a person that controls the person. Furthermore, the spirit of the person that has Godly consciousness as the source will have no problem with libido,

"THE" DIET FOR YOUR MIND TO HELP YOU FIND THE TRUTH THAT WILL SET YOU FREE

erotic or agape love. This is because the mind, having been renewed, is under the control of the author of love, peace and happiness. He is the way the truth and the life.

Since we can be tolerant with outsiders, let us be tolerant with the one who is more a part of our lives. I know the outsiders are not able to hurt as much as a spouse, partner, or friend. We expect more from persons who are close to us.

Well, you want to talk about pain? You want to talk about how a husband, sibling, or partner can cause more pain than a co-worker. Did you not read a few paragraphs above about what Joseph's brothers did to him? Did you not read how Joseph responded; he responded with forgiveness. Being hated by his brothers and sold by his brothers to strangers to be a slave is what Joseph experienced. Yet, Joseph forgave them of their evil act.

I know it's very painful when a member of humanity, whom you identify as of "your race," is the initiator of a painful experience. Well, you just want to get off the comparative pain ride.

Do you remember when I said above that the Manual was good stuff? Also, one of the reasons I found the Manual to be good stuff is because of learning of the life of Jesus. Now, we need to really ask, "What would Jesus do?" Why we ask what would Jesus do is because, Jesus had and has the right stuff to face the pain. While one is mind dieting, just as with physical dieting with exercise, there may be some pain in the effort to gain.

In this life, while in the physical we have to have the right stuff. Not necessarily the Joneses' stuff that we get from trying to keep up with the Joneses, but the good stuff – the spiritual stuff. Remember, what's in the physical is not the true stuff. We can't find out how to respond to experiences in the physical world in the physical. However, I can look to the Spiritual Being who came to the physical and left physical evidence of how to deal with life experiences. To come to a mind like the mind of Christ, to be able to do what Jesus would do, I don't need Tylenoil or aspirin; the stuff I need is the word of God.

Above we have said that Joseph's name was also Israel. The nation of Israel is called Jews. The father of Joseph was Jacob. The Manual says the following:

MALE-FEMALE! HUSBAND-WIFE! AND LOVE

> The book of the generation of Jesus Christ, the Son of David, the son of Abraham. Abraham begat Isaac; and Isaac begat Jacob; and Jacob begat Judas and his brethren; (St. Matthew 1:1,2) [To get the entire line of ancestors, please read the entire first chapter of Matthew.]

The Manual goes on to list each ancestor of Christ, thereby establishing that Jesus was born of Abraham, the promised seed mentioned above and found in the Manual at Genesis 13:14-16. The proof of the ancestors shows that Jesus was a Jew. A further review of the Manual will reveal what his race, the Jews, are accused of doing.

> And as the lame man which was healed held Peter and John, all the people ran together unto them in the porch that is called Solomon's, greatly wondering. And when Peter saw it, he answered unto the people. Ye men of Israel, why look ye so earnestly on us, as though by our own power or holiness we had made this man to walk? The God of Abraham, and of Isaac, and of Jacob, the God of our fathers, hath glorified his Son Jesus; whom ye delivered up, and denied him in the presence of Pilate, when he was determined to let him go. But ye denied the Holy One and the Just, and desired a murderer to be granted unto you; And killed the Prince of life, whom God hath raised from the dead; whereof we are witnesses. (Acts 3:11-15)

> Even in his own land and among his own people, the Jews, he was not accepted. Only a few would welcome and receive him. . . .(St. John 1:11-12 TLB)

We must ask the question, What would Jesus do? And then we must do what Jesus did. Then we will have no problem forgiving. Note that after the Jewish leaders wanted Jesus dead and insisted that he be crucified, he still forgave them before he died.

> Then said Jesus, Father, forgive them; for they know not what they do. And they parted his raiment, and cast lots. (St. Luke 23:34)

As stated before, a person can give, even when they don't like an individual. However, forgiving is most difficult. Forgiving is the most difficult of giving, forgiving and understanding (love), because the self will give out of self or worldly consciousness. But forgiving, which requires the forsaking self, cannot be accomplished. Thus, to close our eyes to what we have seen, and open our hearts fed by a renewed mind, is to find the forgiving that is as Jesus does.

5-FAITH

Finally, we reach the fifth element, which is not only an essential element of man-woman relationships but also the core of Christianity and relationships between God and people. This element is *faith,* faith in God and faith in one another through God.

We have discussed faith above as one of the elements of the Christian Trinity. However, as with forgiveness, we will discuss faith in light of the man-woman relationship. Let us review the definition of faith again.

> What is faith? It is the confident assurance that something we want is going to happen. It is the certainty that what we hope for is waiting for us, even though we cannot see it up ahead. Men of God in days of old were famous for their faith. By faith – by believing in God – we know that the world and the stars – in fact, all things – were at God's command; and that they were all made from things that can't be seen. (Hebrews 11:1—3 TLB)

As we develop faith in God, we come to realize that this is faith in the heavenly Father who knows what is best for us, His children. We must realize that God is the creator of all life. The basis for this statement is found in the first two chapters of Genesis. Although we may say that we are products of our earthly parents, we can't stop at the last, but must go back to the beginning.

The Manual says that in the beginning, God created heaven and earth and all that dwells above, beneath, upon and within. The key in this scripture is He created the seen from things that cannot be seen. The revelation of the unseen quality, which faith is composed of, becomes obvious. To have faith is to believe even before you see. There is a scripture that says we walk by faith and not by sight. So, faith says even when you can't see a way, still believe in a way and there will be a way.

> In reply, Jesus said to the disciples, "If you only have faith in God -this is the absolute truth – you can say to this Mount of Olives, 'Rise up and fall into the Mediterranean,' and your command will be obeyed. All that's required is that you really believe and have no doubt! Listen to me! You can pray for anything, and if you believe, you can have it; it's yours!" (St. Mark 11:22-24 TLB)

The topic of faith has been examined and discussed previously. Here, when we speak of love or marriage having the element of faith, I merely wish to point out that having faith means saying that if God is for the relationship or marriage, who can be against the same? The only potentially successful enemy to the relationship or marriage is oneself. Your greatest potential enemy in this life is the self. Hence, if you do not have faith in God and yourself, neither will anyone else. And God cannot let faith lead you because you will not.

So, when things appear to be what they are not, remember the Father, Son and Holy Ghost indeed are. And when things appear to fall apart, remember, He's got the whole world in His hands. This means you are also in His hands. And by faith, you believe that everything will be all right, with her or him, husband or wife. This belief is rooted in faith in your friend or spouse via faith in the heavenly Father and your big brother, Jesus Christ.

To have faith in your partner is to believe that the two of you through the help, guidance, and blessing of the Supreme Being can overcome all obstacles that may prevent the two of you from becoming as one. Greater is He that is in you than he that is in the world. (I John 4:4) However, when a couple has reached the understanding of friendship, frankness, fidelity and forgiveness, they will have no difficulty in finding faith in the relationship.

We can say, because of faith, when the negative can be seen, the unseen positive is held onto, with the knowledge that all things work together for the good of those who love the Lord, who are in a relationship or marriage according to His purpose. Thus, with faith, we can believe that what God has put together, no man or woman can put asunder.

> Honor Christ by submitting to each other. You wives must submit to your husband's leadership in the same way you submit to the Lord. For a husband is in charge of his wife in the same way Christ is in charge of his body the church. (He gave his very life to take care of it and be its Savior!) So you wives must willingly obey your husbands in everything, just as the church obeys Christ. And you husbands, show the same kind of love to your wives as Christ showed to the church when he died for her,
>
> That is how husbands should treat their wives, loving them as a part of themselves. For since a man and his wife are now one, a man is really doing himself a favor and loving himself when he loves his wife! No one hates his own body but lovingly cares for it, just as Christ cares for his body the church, of which we are parts. (Ephesians 5:21-25; 28-29 TLB)

Today, I know a number of contemporary liberated women who will object to the above scripture that requires submission to the husband. First, let me say, the above is the scripture and not this writer's opinion. Hence, if you desire to get angry, get angry with God and not this writer (the messenger).

Secondly, the scripture is speaking of a marriage wherein both parties are Christians. Inasmuch as the Lord is actually the one in control, the woman has no problem with submitting to the man. However, if you are a Christian and not married or anticipating marriage to a Christian, then you cannot expect the above to be applicable to you. As mentioned above you are unevenly yoked. Hence the "do unto others before they do unto you" philosophy of the non-believer, will never understand or be subjected to "do unto others as you would have them do unto you." Therefore, forgiveness to a non-believer is the same as oil is to water, and we all know the two cannot mix.

However, if you insist on holding this writer responsible for something, then allow me to give you the opportunity. I will take the responsibility for calling on partners and mates to establish some rules or roles that are identifiable for each mate or partner. The role or roles do not have to be assigned according to gender, but they must be identified and understood. The lack of this understanding will lead to disharmony and confusion. The holy understanding that God the Holy Spirit can use any child of God to do the will of God will dispel the assignment according to gender.

> And it shall come to pass in the last days, saith God, I will pour out of my Spirit upon all flesh: and your daughters shall prophesy, and your young men shall see visions, and your old men shall dream dreams. (Acts 2:17)

Recently a co-worker and I were discussing the requirement of roles and the product of the same. The co-worker stated that each worker has a role to perform in the workplace. Thus, if each worker would do or perform his or her role, then the work effort on each part would be easier and the process of developing the product would be more efficient. Immediately I thought of the Holy-Trinity and the identifiable roles the Father, Son and Holy Spirit perform.

We previously said that they (The Father, Son and Holy Spirit) can be called one because, even though they each may have attributes of the other, each has an assigned role and each will do only that which was and is included in each identifiable assigned role.

So, this writer has no problem with Mr. Mom or Mrs. Dad. However, somebody has to perform certain roles. Oh yes, there can be a fifty-fifty role played in any function. Just make sure there is an understanding that the role is shared fifty-fifty.

In the Old Testament, as previously mentioned, God mostly spoke to humanity through man. In the New Testament, in the present days of our lives, as we search for tomorrow, whether we are young and restless, or bold and beautiful, as we seek the guiding light, we will see that, as in Acts 2:17, God no longer relies totally on the male gender and He would say, "I have given the task to all my children".

Finally, a husband who is a Christian will not only call upon his wife to be submissive but would also call to himself the knowledge that his wife really is a part of himself and wouldn't desire harm to himself but would desire love. The Christian husband with his mind

"THE" DIET FOR YOUR MIND TO HELP YOU FIND THE TRUTH THAT WILL SET YOU FREE

on a diet of the Spirit will see himself as an extension of his wife and see roles are needed and gender is not a necessary prerequisite for any identifiable role.

Thus, we could conclude that there is nothing wrong with submissiveness or forgiveness. If there is a problem with one of these, it is because of the mind of the husband, whether the mind is rooted in the scriptures or in the things of the world. The forgiving and the relationship are rooted in faith because the persons involved in the relationship are walking by faith in God through Jesus Christ.

With faith, friendship is established, a friendship of love, giving, forgiving and understanding. With faith persons are able to be frank and communicate freely with each other because truth will stand as a house built on a rock. Yes, the wind will come, shaking prior belief, the floods will come, there will be a need for change, and the rain will descend on your parade. However, when life is based upon frankness and truth, it – the relationship – will survive.

With faith, fidelity will be no problem. As one contemplates going to another to find the missing link, one will realize that what God has joined together cannot be joined together any better. Therefore, just as one would go to God, and have no other before Him, the person would go to their spouse, or friend, to keep the relationship in tact.

With faith the mountain of pain that sometimes has to be experienced when forgiving would be endured until the pain is cast into the sea, because Jesus has shown that this is the way, the truth and normal experiences of life. Finally, as a born-again believer, you recognize that you have hope in the relationship or marriage, and faith is the substance – the foundation – for which you hope. The hope and faith are based upon the knowledge that God created the family. God cares so much about the family that He sent His only begotten son to die so the Godly and human family could exist again. Hence, the partners (male and female) have a holy understanding that God the father, Son and Holy Spirit will keep the family together.

PARENT-CHILD LOVE

The child also provides an example of true love. A child is born into this world and the parents give to the child according to its needs and more. Yet, parents ask for nothing in return. The parents experience joy and happiness, which are derived from the act of giving.

Later, as the child is growing up, he or she does something wrong, tells a lie, or gets into legal trouble. No matter what the child does, good parents will be there throughout the child's life, whether the child is a saint or a sinner, still giving, forgiving, and understanding, because of love.

If a child breaks a dish at home, the parents may get upset, but they will forgive the child. If he breaks a neighbor's window or a window at home, the child may get a scolding and be told that money doesn't grow on trees. However, the parents will forgive the child. Transgressions or violations of man's law may cause the parents to be embarrassed along with having to spend money, yet the parents will forgive the child. We know there are exceptions to the rule, but seldom do you find a parent abandoning the child because of embarrassment or monetary cost. The parents are there regardless of the cost in terms of money or community embarrassment.

Furthermore, a parent is protective of its child. He or she may be the ugliest child on the block, but to the parents, he or she is beautiful. His or her moral standards or ethics may fall short of the norm, yet the child is defended to the end.

Within the relationship, we find that the parents understand the child. This understanding is based partially on the interaction of the family. Parents will say things, from their understanding, such as, "Well, he's like his father," "She got it from her mother," "He or she is like this or that, but he or she is mine."

Often an outsider or a mere observer will respond to these statements by parents as rationalizations or excuses. But who are they to judge? Maybe there is something that is not consistent with the standards set in a child's life that was inherited from or learned from the parents. Furthermore, we must admit that as a parent, we do, or have done, the same things at some time. Nevertheless, regardless of the authenticity of the explanations, the point being emphasized here is that the parents do have understanding. Thus, we are able to find within the family the giving, forgiving and understanding, which are the summation of what we call agape love.

A problem surfaces in the parent-child relationship when the child grows older. When the child begins to think for himself or herself and make decisions contrary to the parent's instructions or guidance, we find giving, forgiving, and understanding by the parents a thing of the past. Please, parents, be constantly aware that children learn from examples. They will be guided by the examples you, their peers, their teachers and life in general provide. Thus, the interaction between parent and child will have an impact on the child's life. It will provide the examples that they learn from and will be the source from which they draw their knowledge as they travel in life. In other words, if you are a giving, forgiving and understanding parent, your offspring will be the same.

In seminars, where I teach on family and marriage, there is one piece of advice I share with participants. In all interactions, whether between husband and wife, friend and friend, or parent and child, each party should say to the other, "Meet me at the cross." In other words, let's not build a relationship of dominance. Let not one friend control the other or a parent controlling because they are the parents or adults. Rather, let the relationship be vested in what Jesus would say and what Jesus would do or have us do in the relationship. Even though the Manual says, "Woman, submit yourself unto your husband, and, children, honor and obey your parents," the relationship must follow other scriptures. It should follow scriptures such as, "Husband love your wife as yourself (Ephesians 5:28), and, parents, don't be harsh with your children (Ephesians 6:4)." These are also to be taken into consideration.

The point is drawn from the fact that many husbands neglect the feeling of their wives on the basis of being the masculine gender. Many parents neglect to listen, seek understanding of their children on the basis of being an adult or the head of the children. Therefore, their relationship is not based totally in Christ but on position.

Jesus held the position of being the only begotten Son, the maker of all things and the holder of all power. Yet, He submitted to the will of the Father, accepted ridicule from the Pharisees and Sadducees and gave His life for our sins, even though He never committed any sin. Hence, in spite of His position, He gave, forgave and exercised understanding. He became a servant; when according to the position He held, He should have been served. He allowed Himself to be taken into custody, to stand trial in a mockery of a court and to be whipped all night long, given a thorny crown upon His head, nailed to the cross, pierced in the side and stripped of clothing to die a shameful death because of His position and because of love. In spite of holding a position, which should not have allowed these occurrences He accepted the same.

This is why I urge parents not to use position when relating to their children, but to use Christ. We cannot tell our children to do as we say because we are the parents without our children reminding us that even parents make mistakes. Hence, position is not the answer, but Jesus is the answer. Thus, parents are seeking the will of God. Children are seeking the will of God. Then God, not position, is the sustainer of the relationship. God says, "Do unto others as you would have them do unto you." This golden rule applies not only to adult-to-adult relations, but also to relations between adult and child.

When the above is followed, the parent understands and nothing stops them from giving to the child and forgiving the child even though the child is subject to the authority of the parent.

Children, the same Bible that requests parents not to be harsh to their children also says, "Honor they mother and father." In other words, obey thy parents.

Ephesians 6:1—3 (TLB) says:
> Children, obey your parents; this is the right thing to do because God has placed them in authority over you. Honor your father and mother. This is the first of God's Ten Commandments that ends with a promise. And this is the promise: that if you honor your father and mother, yours will be a long life, full of blessings.

You see, Mom and Dad have traveled the same road you travel right now. Thus, from their experiences, they can guide you along the

"THE" DIET FOR YOUR MIND TO HELP YOU FIND THE TRUTH THAT WILL SET YOU FREE

way. Understand that what you desire may not be the best for you. Learn how to talk to your parents. Learn that it's not what you say, but how you say it. "I ain't washing dishes" or "They won't let me go out" are not proper responses. Be understanding and learn how to talk to your parents and others, young and old, so you'll be able to communicate with them. Furthermore, whom would you prefer to lead you to a place you've never been? Would you prefer a person like yourself, who has never been there, or a person who has traveled there before? I know that you agree that the one with experience would be better prepared to lead. He or she would know all the possible obstacles and all the possible snares, and could prepare you for what lies ahead.

The older members of the family are to be the leaders because of their experiences. This is why God placed them over the children. Well, that's not the way it is in actuality. Could it be that our parents don't help us because instead of working with them, we see them as an obstacle. Therefore, instead of seeking their wisdom, we seek ways to oppose them. Before we criticize our parents, we must first find out what they have lived through. Then maybe we'll understand their attitudes and be a little less hostile and more understanding. Honor thy mother and father that your days will be longer.

I know that parents aren't always what they should be. You say, "They hate me; they don't care about me; they don't love me." I am sure you feel that you are right. They don't love you or care for you. That's why they sit up with you when you are ill as an infant, adolescent, or adult. That's why they provide you with food, shelter and clothing for at least eighteen years. That's why, even though they may not have gone to college, they send you there. That's why they buy you musical instruments, cars to drive, and are always there with a loan. That's why when you have a problem, they talk to you and help you find a solution.

I see exactly what you mean. I guess they should die for you, and then you would believe they love you, for this would be the proof of their love. But wait, wasn't there a young man some 2,000 years ago, a Nazarene who died for our sins and said He did so because He loved us? What was His name? Jesus – Jesus Christ. But we don't believe in Him or love as He and the Father commanded us.

PARENT-CHILD LOVE

It's time for us to remember that so many have done so much for us. We can begin with our parents. Parents are busy and sometimes fail to see our needs or problems. There is a communication problem in most homes. Close evaluation and open-mindedness will certainly cure all your misconceptions about parents. They are human. They may not make the same mistakes as you, but they are learning. Maybe if you and your parents both read the section on each other, you will all see that there are not really bad children and there are not really unconcerned parents. Remember, as the song said, "We're all in this thing together, and we've got to work it out."

When parents chastise us, they mean well. For the Bible says, "Spare the rod and spoil the child." There are two basic actions that can affect our emotions – love and hate. Consider the persons you can remember readily. These are people who affect you in a negative or positive way. The neutral people (the ones you neither hate nor love) seldom enter your mind and are hard for you to remember. But if you love the person, the name brings the image of this person quickly into focus.

I am saying this because, as I have said, your parents do too many things for you to hate you. Therefore, they must love you. The punishment you may receive is not out of hatred but out of love. In love, giving is not always the giving of pleasant advice or information. It is the giving of what is needed.

I could never understand why, when my brother would dare me to do something, my mother would chastise me (whip my rear) for challenging the dare. "Why?" I asked myself. She didn't love me, I decided. My brother should have received the chastising. But, as I grew older, I finally realized why. You see if I were to live my life challenging dares, it would certainly be cut short. What do I mean? Perhaps if someone held a weapon aimed at my forehead and dare me to move, if I were to challenge the dare, the probability of my staying alive even to do this writing would be less. However, I have learned not necessarily to give up challenging a dare, but to always calculate the risks to my safety.

I said discipline is an act of love. The Bible gives permission for discipline by our earthly parents as well as our heavenly Father:

"THE" DIET FOR YOUR MIND TO HELP YOU FIND THE TRUTH THAT WILL SET YOU FREE

> And have you quite forgotten the encouraging words God spoke to you, his child? He said, "My son, don't be angry when the Lord punishes you. Don't be discouraged when he has to show you that you are wrong. For when he punishes you, it proves that he loves you. When he whips you it proves that you are really his child." Let God train you, for he is doing what any loving father does for his children. Whoever heard of a son who was never corrected? If God doesn't punish you when you need it, as other fathers punish their sons, then it means that you aren't really God's son at all – that you don't really belong in his family. Since we respect our fathers here on earth, though they punish us, should we not all the more cheerfully submit to God's training so that we can begin really to live? Our earthly fathers trained us for a few brief years, doing the best for us that they knew how, but God's correction is always right and for our best good, that we may share his holiness. Being punished isn't enjoyable while it is happening – it hurts! But afterwards we can see the result, a quiet growth in grace and character. (Hebrews 12:5-11 TLB)

Discipline and chastisement are done so you will be a producer as opposed to a spiritual and social non-producer. In St. John 15:1-2, Jesus speaks of pruning the branch (offspring) so that it will produce. If you are not disciplined, you will be useless to yourself, your family and God. Hence, the right attitude when we are disciplined is to accept all that is done as for our benefit.

Finally, if you are a Christian, stop being ashamed of being a young Christian. We have come a long way in accepting sex as part of our life, so why not do the same with Christianity. Furthermore, just as we did with sex, if the stigma is eliminated and we openly confess that it's cool or hip to be a Christian, maybe our friends will do the same. To be a Christian is nothing to be ashamed of. In fact, we should be glad to be able to identify with our Father, the Son, and the Holy Spirit. When you confess with your mouth that Jesus is Lord of your life, the belief in your heart will be strengthened. Let your

PARENT-CHILD LOVE

friends know about your partner, Jesus, and the many miracles he has provided and will provide for you and them.

Religion with me used to be a very private thing. My acceptance of His calling also brought along with it openness and willingness to be viewed by others in the light of my belief. But religion is like love; it's not really worthwhile until it is shared with others. Furthermore, Christianity is more than a religion. Christianity is a way of life.

I know you are afraid that you will lose some of your friends when and if you openly confess Jesus. Remember this: if a person can't accept you and your belief, that person is not really your friend. However, if you lose a friend, God will replace that friend with several others. This is stated in the scripture at Mark 10:28-30 TLB:

> Then Peter began to mention all that he and the other disciples had left behind. "We've given up everything to follow you," he said. And Jesus replied, "Let me assure you that no one has given up anything – home, brothers, sisters, mother, father, children or property – for love of me and to tell others the Good News, who won't be given back, a hundred times over, homes, brothers, sisters, mothers, children and land – with persecutions!" All these will be his here on earth, and in the world to come he shall have eternal life.

Love is giving and sharing, forgiving and continuing sharing, and understanding and going forward, sharing with others. Your parents gave, to and for you, before you could do for yourself. Accepting them as parents and being obedient to the word of God can demonstrate a recognition and appreciation of their love. Children, honor thy mother and father and love them with all your heart.

There are a number of books that parents and children should read. These writings may share with the parents things they already know. However, the writing may give a new or different approach to parents and children communicating in the parent-child relationship. Furthermore, we have learned that relationships between adult and child or adult and adult can only exist when there is giving, forgiving and understanding (love).

"THE" DIET FOR YOUR MIND TO HELP YOU FIND THE TRUTH THAT WILL SET YOU FREE

IS LOVE A STRENGTH OR WEAKNESS?

Is love a strength or weakness? When this question enters my mind, several other questions enter, and the conclusions are all the same.

The preceding chapters have given the definition of love and all its attributes. If one has come to the plateau of understanding love, then one has to agree that love is a strength. However, some people (particularly males) see love as a weakness. Therefore, if love is seen as a weakness, and God is love, they see God as a weakling. In other words, they reject God and love with the same breath. However, regardless of their rationalizations and explanations, if they don't know God they cannot love. Oh, they may say they love, they may demonstrate some signs of love, or they may actually believe they have loved. But, how can they love, when you must believe in love in order to have it? Hence, if one believes in God, one believes in love. If one believes in love, one believes in God. If you have a friend that has not accepted God, and does not know God, whether he or she calls Him, Jehovah or Allah, this person does not know love. The reason is because love is another name for God.

As with love, many see believing in God as a weakness. They see tears (especially from men) as a symbol of weakness. (Oh, do my brothers perish from a lack of knowledge.) If they were to read the Holy Bible, as they read Playboy, or in addition to reading Playboy, at St. John 11:32-35, they would see that Jesus cried.

> Then when Mary was come to where Jesus was, and saw Him, she fell down at His feet, saying unto Him, Lord, if thou hadst been here, my brother had not died. When Jesus therefore saw her weeping, and the Jews also weeping which came with her, He groaned in the spirit, and was troubled, And said, Where have ye laid him? They said unto him, Lord come and see. Jesus wept.

Yes, Jesus cried. Jesus' crying does not mean that all Christians or believers in God should always cry. Rather it clarifies the misunderstanding many have about certain human behavior. The

IS LOVE A STRENGTH OR WEAKNESS?

human behavior of crying is not a weakness. Sometimes when I experience deep or constant laughter, my eyes run with tears of joy. Have you ever seen a joyous person? The tears run down his or her face, as water would flow from a faucet. Hence, there is such a thing as tears of joy. As the scripture says, all sickness is not unto death. Nor is illness the result of sin. All tears are not because of pain or suffering.

Christ's tears referred to above are tears shed because of the deep compassion, sympathy, and empathy felt by Jesus. I believe He was crying not only because of Lazarus' death, but because He had to call Lazarus back to this sin-sick world. This Lazarus, the brother of Mary and Martha, was probably in the bosom of Abraham, as was Lazarus the beggar. Abraham's bosom, as described in St Luke 16:19-25, is a place of comfort. It is a place of comfort where the beggar after dying received comfort, whereas in this world he begged for crumbs from the rich man's table. Thus, to bring Mary and Martha's brother, Lazarus, back from the comfort of Abraham's bosom caused a hurt so deep that Jesus wept. Yet Jesus is God and God was Jesus in the flesh.

> Before anything else existed, there was always Christ, with God. He has always been alive and is himself God. And Christ became a human being and lived here on earth among us and was full of loving forgiveness and truth. (St. John 1:1-2,14 TLB)

Even if you stop short of accepting Jesus as God, you have to recognize that He was and is the Son of God:

> And Jesus, when He was baptized, went up straightway out of the water: and, lo, the heavens were opened up unto Him, and He saw the Spirit of God descending like a dove, and lighting upon Him: And lo a voice from heaven, saying, This is my beloved Son, in whom I am well pleased. (St. Matthew 3:16-17)

And since He is God, He had and has all power in Heaven and earth.

He has power:

> Thinkest thou that I cannot now pray to My Father, and He shall presently give Me more than twelve legions of angels? (St. Matthew 26:53)

And Jesus came and spake with unto them, saying, All power is given unto me in heaven and in earth. (St. Matthew 28:18)

He has the power over sin:

Jesus could read their minds and said to them at once, "Why does this bother you? I, the Messiah, have the authority on earth to forgive sins. But talk is cheap – anybody could say that. So I'll prove it to you by healing this man." Then turning to the paralyzed man, he commanded, "Pick up your stretcher and go on home, for you are healed." (St. Mark 2:8-11 TLB)

He has power over disease:

Look! A leper is approaching. He kneels before Him, worshipping. "Sir," the leper pleads, "if you want to, you can heal me." Jesus touches the man, "I want to," He says. "Be healed,." And instantly the leprosy disappears. (St. Matthew 8:2-3 TLB)

He has power over paralysis:

When Jesus arrived in Capernaum, a Roman army captain came and pled with Him to come to his home and heal his servant boy who was in bed paralyzed and racked with pain. Then Jesus said to the Roman officer, "Go on home. What you have believed has happened!" And the boy was healed that same hour! (St. Matthew 8:5, 6 & 13)

He has power over illness:

When Jesus arrived at Peter's house, Peter's mother-in-law was in bed with a high fever. But when Jesus touched her hand, the fever left her; and she got up and prepared a meal for them! (St. Matthew 8:14-15 TLB)

He has power over demons (evil):

That evening several demon-possessed people were brought to Jesus; and when he spoke a single word, all the demons fled; and all the sick were healed. (St. Matthew 8:16 TLB)

IS LOVE A STRENGTH OR WEAKNESS?

He has power over nature:
> Then He got into a boat and started across the lake with His disciples. Suddenly a terrible storm came up, with waves higher than the boat. But Jesus was asleep. The disciples went to him and wakened him, shouting, "Lord, save us! We're sinking!" But Jesus answered, "O, you men of little faith! Why are you so frightened?" Then he stood up and rebuked the wind and the waves, and the storm subsided and all was calm. (St. Matthew 8:23-26 TLB)

And he has power over death:
> Six days before the Passover ceremonies began, Jesus arrived in Bethany where Lazarus was – the man he had brought back to life. (St. John 12:1 TLB)

Now since Jesus has all of this power, if He cried, does that make Him weak? I would think the answer is quite the contrary. Love between a man and woman is considered a weakness. Hence, some men will deny themselves of the greatest force on earth. To love is to know power. It takes more strength to discipline oneself and not return an eye for an eye, and a tooth for a tooth, than to act out these phrases.

To love your enemy – to give to, forgive and understand your enemy – takes more strength than ignoring, denying them and forgetting them. When will we realize that true strength does not sleep with weapons but rather with the inner self? Jesus came and conquered the hearts and minds of many during His walk on earth. He conquers the hearts of millions even today. Nowhere in the scriptures can you find that He used physical force or weapons. What did Jesus use to conquer? He used love. Even when betrayed by one of His inner circle of followers (Judas), when the other disciples sought to defend Him with a weapon, He condemned their use of the weapon. This is because He knew that those who live by the sword will perish by the sword.

> Then said Jesus unto him, Put up again thy sword into his place: for all they that take the sword shall perish with the sword. (St. Matthew 26:52)

"THE" DIET FOR YOUR MIND TO HELP YOU FIND THE TRUTH THAT WILL SET YOU FREE

I know that you probably think that I sound like a believer in unilateral disarmament by the United States. I'm not an expert in foreign affairs or defense. However, I know that the U.S. and the former U.S.S.R. will never come to love each other because they don't have a friendship, frankness, fidelity, forgiveness, or faith in one another. Hence, they could never love. But why should I concern myself with washing a truck, when I can't wash a car? The point is, we need to learn how to love each other, before we consider the actions of a group, the United States, and a group of people called Russians. We need to understand the source of strength and not continue to believe that weapons made by man are stronger than the creator of man. There is strength in turning the other cheek, giving to enemies, and having compassion and understanding for others. If you reject this strength, maybe you don't understand love. Therefore, it's not love that is weak but you who are so weak. You cannot muster up enough courage to try something different. Hence, you go through life blaspheming God, the world and others for your failures. And your biggest failure is the failure to see through God's eyes, hear with God's ears, and think as God thinks. This can only be done through a fellowship with God through Jesus Christ. Again, you fail to accept God, and in so doing you fail to accept love.

CONCLUSION

The dessert, love, was saved for the last, because it is the foundation of the diet for the mind. It was sin that caused the separation of humanity from God and the need for the mind diet. It is love that created the possibility of reuniting humanity with God. These truths must be eaten and digested. Without this truth, humanity can never be free. The truth of how the soul became contaminated, and the need for an antidote, was presented to acknowledge that, "Houston (Humanity), we have a problem!"

The solution to the problem was to get a Holy Understanding. The Holy understanding presented above continued from the contamination, its origin and so on, to understanding why, how and so on. The awakening of conscience, the awareness of good and evil led to the need for humanity to ingest good and refuse to consume evil. Thus, the need for the right stuff arose; after all there is all kind of stuff out there to be consumed. We found the right stuff in the Manual, The Holy Bible. The Manual became a lamp to humanity's feet, a light to guide humanity on the path of righteousness.

The need for the recognition and activation of the sixth sense became a cornerstone for the diet when seeking the truth that will set you free. The awareness of the sixth sense brought the truth that one cannot depend on the five senses, because of the contamination (virus) in the PCS. Furthermore, to get the sixth sense, which is the only way to eradicate the virus, there had to be a second birth. After the second birth (being born-again) came the ability to see the truth and live in truth.

We discovered that Moses gave Ten Commandments and Jesus, the anti-virus, summed them up in two commandments; love God and love your fellow person. Thus, even though love has been identified as the dessert in the diet for the mind, when Holy understanding is established, the sixth sense reveals that love is not to be consumed last; rather, is the reason for all. Thus, love is in the first as well as all the other courses in this eight-course diet for the mind to find the truth that will set you free.

"THE" DIET FOR YOUR MIND TO HELP YOU FIND THE TRUTH THAT WILL SET YOU FREE

The words contained in this writing are presented to help us understand what love is and what love has got to do with it. As I pondered to find a word or words to summarize this writing, the spirit led me to some words that will never pass away. These words are my hope, my faith, my joy, and my peace. These words speak of the true love, a love that is not restricted or influenced by human emotions. The words that you can sink your teeth into are words that can be found in the word of God.

> Who then can ever keep Christ's love from us? When we have trouble or calamity, when we are hunted down or destroyed, is it because He doesn't love us anymore? And if we are hungry, or penniless, or in danger, or threatened with death, has God deserted us? No, for the Scriptures tell us that for His sake we must be ready to face death at every moment of the day – we are like sheep awaiting slaughter; but despite all this, overwhelming victory is ours through Christ who loved us enough to die for us. For I am convinced that nothing can ever separate us from His love. Death can't, and life can't. The angels won't, and all the powers of hell itself cannot keep God's love away. Our fears for today, our worries about tomorrow, or where we are –high above the sky, or in the deepest ocean – nothing will ever be able to separate us from the love of God demonstrated by our Lord Jesus Christ when He died for us. (Romans 8:35-40) TLB

We often say to someone whom we love, but for some reason we must be separated from, "I will never forget you, I'll always love you, I will always think of you, and if you need me, call me." Then as time passes and new days, months, years and people come and go, someone else receives our love. Thus, we forget our promise. However, with God this is not true. That is why God is so big; He has to have a heart big enough to love all of us. He can't forget us because the slain lamb (Jesus) sits next to Him on the throne constantly reminding the Father (God) of the price He paid for our acceptance and God's promise that He will always love us.

CONCLUSION

Thus this writing has attempted to help us understand that all creation began with the spiritual. Therefore, if we are to understand what love is or what love has got to do with it, we must first understand the love of God. This love (the love of God) is our genesis, our foundation for all love, which includes emotional love. Emotional love can be as enduring as spiritual love, provided that the emotions are rooted in and grow from spiritual love.

The selfishness, which is a part of our nature, prevents or may interfere with the greater true self, the universal self, which is God. Hence, we had to go beyond human examples and representations of love. We had to remove the soil that covered the truth. We had to bypass the smaller roots just beneath the immediate surface, which were signs of the real source but did not reveal it. We had to find the taproot, the main artery, the reason the tree exists.

The cause, the reason, the explanation, is the truth that will make us free. It will make us free from selfishness, physical hang-ups, pride, self-pity and the deceit of this world. Hence, when you believe in God the Father and Jesus the Son, you have to accept that such false indications as tingling in the toes, a fluttering of the heart, a weakness in the knees (emotions in general) are not the answer. The physical may look good, but it may not be good for us. However, God loves us, not only through words but also through acts. In other words, God can say that He shows and tells. He has shown us by giving us His Son. He has told us through His word.

This writing has attempted to address the common or expected questions and circumstances around love. The rock upon which the words are built is the second person in the Holy Trinity, Jesus Christ. Someone may say that they have found love according to the formula and explanation given herein. But this does not make them a Christian. Furthermore, there are Jews who practice Judaism, Orientals who practice Buddhism and Muslims who practice Islam who have found love. Nevertheless, they are not Christians. Hence, how can this writer claim that finding love can only be accomplished through knowing Jesus Christ?

One lesson I have learned from life is that credit often falls upon a person who has not earned it. In churches, there are Christians who have heard the preaching and teaching of God through their pastor or a minister. These Christians have a greater affection for that pastor or minister than they have for God.

There are people who advance in their employment and give the credit to a supervisor or a person who "put in a good word." Then we have those who learn a solution from another and then share the solution with others. Thus, the originator is omitted. The point is that one may have learned or experienced the necessary elements of love without recognizing their origin.

Those who have experienced love who believe not in Christianity but some other religion, please remember that this writer stated that love has to be found in the spiritual. The one who taught me love and its elements is the one who came from the spiritual and took on the flesh. Therefore, He receives the credit. The means by which others learn love, I cannot say. However, when I consider other religions, I notice that they are similar to Christianity. The main difference is their denial of the son-ship of Jesus and refusal to accept Him as the Messiah, as the Son of God. They say He's a great teacher and a good man, even a prophet. Therefore, they refuse to accept Him as the sacrificial lamb. Thus, they or their basic religion could be within the teachings of Christ even though they do not accept Him. Therefore, they accept and follow another who has taught according to Jesus. The main reservation I have in accepting an individual's claim to have agape love without Christ is that the individual has not been born-again. Furthermore, if Jesus is not their sacrificial lamb, then who or what is their sacrificial lamb? Whose blood was shed for their sins? Does a mother's denial that a son is his father's refute the truth that he is the father's? Does the refusal to accept a person as equal or as a fellow human because of race or color negate the fact that the person is a human being? No, whether something is or is not will not depend upon its acceptance. The same is true of love and Jesus Christ. Many have rejected His son-ship, but do accept and practice His teachings. Thus, the credit is due whether it is given or not.

Furthermore, once you have sincerely sought and carried out the elements of love you will know that the elements mentioned herein are the substance of true love. You'll know that Jesus is love. Furthermore, you'll know that the finding of love in the spiritual is the beginning of physical appreciation of fellow humans, whether children, spouses, friends, or just fellow human beings.

The question for you now is not, What's love got to do with it? Nor, do you need to know what love is? The question is, Will you seek true love – giving and forgiving through understanding? Will you seek true love or will you settle for a thrill? And we know that if the thrill is your gnosis, sooner or later you will cry the thrill is gone. Hence, the thrill is temporary but the love found in the spiritual is everlasting.

Therefore, the thrill is the icing, but the spiritual is the cake. It is my heart's desire that you have the icing but I know you need a cake to build your icing upon. May God bless you through His love.

Now the end of the commandment is charity out of a pure heart, and of a pure conscience, and of faith unfeigned: (1 Timothy 1:5)

What I am eager for is that all the Christians there will be filled with love that comes from pure hearts, and that their minds will be clean and their faith strong. (1 Timothy 1:5 TLB)

"THE" DIET FOR YOUR MIND TO HELP YOU FIND THE TRUTH THAT WILL SET YOU FREE

FOOTNOTES AND SOURCES

INTRODUCTION
[1] The scripture quotes were taken from *The Scofield Study Bible*, previously published as *The Scofield Reference Bible*. New York: Oxford University Press, 1909, 1917, 1937, and 1945

[2] "TLB" after a scripture quote means the scripture was taken from *The Living Bible*. Wheaton, Illinois: Pydale House Publisher, 1971

THE MIND
[1] All word definitions were taken from *Webster's New World Dictionary, Compact School and Office Edition.* Cleveland and New York: Collins and World Publishing Co. Inc., 1974

WISDOM KNOWLEDGE and "HOLY" UNDERSTANDING
[1] Scofield, supra

LUCIFER
[1] Scofield, 1350, footnote number 2

THE TRINITY OF CONSCIOUSNESS
[1] Scofield, 1200, footnote number 1

THE SECOND BIRTH (BORN-AGAIN)
[1] Scofield, 1003
[2] Scofield, 1117
[3] Scofield, ibid

LOVE AND RELATIONSHIPS
[1] Settle, Oscar G., *Love and Relationships,* 2nd printing. New Jersey: 1990

WHAT IS LOVE
[1] The Foreigners, *I Want to Know What Love Is*. New York: Atlantic Recording Corp., 1984

FOOTNOTES AND SOURCES

[2]The New Jersey Mass Choir, *I Want to Know What Love Is*. Elizabeth: Savoy Records, Inc., 1985
[3]Tina Turner, *What's Love Got To Do With It*. U.S.A.: Capitol Records, Inc., 1984

THE ESSENCE OF LOVE
[1]Martin Luther King, Jr., *Strength to Love*. Philadelphia: Fortress Press, 1983, pp. 50, 51-53

LOVE AND LIKE
[1]Paul Tillich, *Love, Power and Justice*. New York: Oxford University Press, 1960
[2]Ibid, p. 26
[3]Ibid, p. 27
[4]Ibid, p. 58
[5]King, *Strength to Love*
[6]Ibid

FIRST CORINTHIANS THIRTEEN
[1]U.S. Andersen, *Secret of Secrets*. New York: Thomas Nelson & Sons, 1976

WHAT'S LOVE GOT TO DO WITH IT
[1]Jackie DeShannon, *What the World Needs Now*. Hollywood: Imperial Records, 1965
[2]Marvin Gaye, *What's Going On*. Detroit: Motown Records Corp., 1971
[3]Marvin Gaye, *Sexual Healing*. New York: Columbia Records, 1982

BROTHERLY AND DIVINE LOVE
[1]*Encyclopedia Dictionary of Religion*. Washington, D.C.: Corpus Publication, 1979, Volume 1, pp. 1229-1230
[2]Ibid, p.70
[3]Ibid

"THE" DIET FOR YOUR MIND TO HELP YOU FIND THE TRUTH THAT WILL SET YOU FREE

[4]Charles F. Stanley, "Family Responsibilities." In *Touch Magazine,* February, 1985, p.12

MALE-FEMALE/HUSBAND-WIFE and LOVE
[1]Paul Tillich, *Love, Power and Justice.* New York: Oxford University Press, 1960

ABOUT THE AUTHOR

Minister Oscar G. Settle is not only a teacher of the Word of God; he is also a licensed attorney at law in the State of Texas. I believe that this dual training background is an enhancer and is a partial reason why he is able to understand the facts of life and through the guidance of the Holy Spirit teach the Word according to the spirit of life existence.

However, all of Minister Settle's training, teaching at various seminars, workshops, and conventions are only possible because of the relationship he has with God through Jesus by the help of the Holy Spirit.

CPSIA information can be obtained
at www.ICGtesting.com
Printed in the USA
FSHW04n0807160318
45795FS